British Mythology

British Mythology

DON NARDO

LUCENT BOOKS
A part of Gale, Cengage Learning

GALE
CENGAGE Learning·

Detroit • New York • San Francisco • New Haven, Conn • Waterville, Maine • London

LIBRARY OF CONGRESS CATALOGING-IN-PUBLICATION DATA

Nardo, Don, 1947-
British mythology / by Don Nardo.
    p. cm. -- (Mythology and culture worldwide)
Includes bibliographical references and index.
ISBN 978-1-4205-0833-8 (hardcover)
1. Mythology, British--Juvenile literature. I. Title.
BL980.G7N37 2013
398.20941--dc23

2012026502

Lucent Books
27500 Drake Rd.
Farmington Hills, MI 48331

ISBN-13: 978-1-4205-0833-8
ISBN-10: 1-4205-0833-4

Printed in the United States of America
1 2 3 4 5 6 7 16 15 14 13 12

TABLE OF CONTENTS

Map of Roman Britain

Roman control

Celtic control

Roman roads

CALEDONIA

Hadrian's Wall

NORTH SEA

Belfast

IRISH SEA

Eboracum

Lindum

BRITANNIA

Camulodunum

Verulamium

Glevum

Londinium

Map of Anglo-Saxon Britain c. 800 CE

Map of Modern Britain

Major Entities in British Mythology

Character Name	Pronunciation	Description
Andraste	(an-DRAH-stee)	A Roman-Celtic war goddess.
Arthur	(AR-ther)	A famous mythical English king who held court in the castle of Camelot.
Bedivere	(BED-uh-veer)	One of King Arthur's most trusted knights.
Beowulf	(BAY-uh-wolf)	The Anglo-Saxon hero who slew the monster Grendel.
Bran	(BRAWN)	A Welsh god who saved his sister Branwen from the clutches of an evil Irish king.
Branwen	(BRAWN-wen or BRAN-oo-wen)	A Welsh goddess who married an Irish king who ended up abusing her.
Culhwch	(kil-HOOKH)	An ancient Welsh hero who had to perform a series of difficult tasks in order to win the hand of the woman he loved.
Grendel	(GREN-dl)	A monster that terrorized the court of King Hrothgar in the story of Beowulf.
Guinevere	(GWEN-uh-veer)	The wife of King Arthur and queen of Camelot.
Hrothgar	(ROTH-gar)	The king who was plagued by the monster Grendel and received help from Beowulf.
Lancelot	(LAN-si-lot)	One of the greatest knights of King Arthur's Round Table. He betrayed Arthur by having an affair with the queen.
Matholwch	(math-OH-lookh)	A wicked Irish king who mistreated his new bride Branwen.
Merlin	(MER-lin)	The mysterious magician who tutored the young King Arthur.
Olwen	(AHL-wen)	The woman with whom the hero Culhwch fell in love and wished to marry.
Thrym	(THRIM or TREEM)	The dim-witted giant who stole the god Thunor's hammer and was severely punished for that crime.
Thunor	(THOO-nor)	The Anglo-Saxon god of thunder, equivalent to the Norse deity Thor.
Uther Pendragon	(OO-ther PEN-drag'n)	The ancient mythical king who ruled England before his son, Arthur.
Woden	(WOH-din)	The leader of the Anglo-Saxon gods, equivalent to the Norse deity Odin.

A Rich, Diverse Mythical Heritage

The mythology of early Britain is one of the richest collections of ancient myths in the world. First, unlike ancient Egypt and Greece, which each had a native population made up mostly of a single cultural and linguistic group, ancient and medieval Britain featured a melting pot of several separate peoples. Each had its own language, customs, histories, gods, and myths. Over time these diverse mythologies sometimes mingled, so that the residents of Britain perpetuated collections of myths having wildly dissimilar origins, characters, and themes.

From Fairies to Heroes

Bygone Britain also had a number of different *types* of myth, each stressing a different aspect of early British life and legend. Some myths told of magical or supernatural beings and happenings, for instance. An example is the rich compilation of old British tales of fairies. These beings, who were mostly bigger and scarier than Walt Disney's cutesy Tinker Bell, were often referred to collectively as Fairy Folk. "Eating their food could make a human their prisoner," British scholar Geoffrey Ashe explains.

They were fond of dancing, especially in circles. At night a wanderer might catch a glimpse of their revels and probably have cause to regret it. . . . They could be mischievous, and far worse than mischievous. They were apt to steal away children for breeding purposes, and leave substitutes or changelings who were stunted, strange, [or] disturbing. When angry, they might use magical powers to inflict disease. . . . Yet they could [also] be benevolent. They might live unseen in a fireplace and help with housework, so long as the fireplace was kept clean for them.[1]

Another kind of British myth consisted of mainly invented tales designed to fill the many and sometimes large gaps in the histories of local regions. These stories often featured the founders of cities or the rulers of early kingdoms. The King Arthur legends are a well-known example, as is the tale of King Leir. In King Leir's story, as an old man he seeks

The fairies of British folklore were known for night revels of dancing and mischief making, such as stealing children and inflicting illness, but they could also be generous and do good.

to divide his kingdom among his three daughters, but two of them turn on him with tragic results. So compelling is this myth that many centuries later the renowned English playwright William Shakespeare used it as the basis for *King Lear*, which is still widely deemed one of the greatest plays ever written.

Still another category of British myth explored the exploits of some of the early Christian saints who dwelled in Britain. One of the most famous was Saint George, said to have been a Roman soldier who converted to Christianity. According to legend, when Rome's emperor demanded that George renounce his Christian beliefs, the soldier refused, so the emperor had him executed. Before this episode, however, George supposedly slew a dragon that was going to kill a young maiden and also visited England. The English became so fond of him that they later adopted him as a patron saint and designated April 23 as a holiday in his honor.

Most prominent of all were the stories of mythical heroes, tales that dominate the existing corpus (body or collection) of British myths. These memorable figures range from the hardy monster slayer Beowulf to the even more renowned King Arthur and Robin Hood. Bigger than life, each has been the focus of numerous written stories over the centuries, and new versions of literary portrayals of these figures routinely continue to appear today.

Tales Memorized and Recited

At first, however, the heroes' tales and the other British myths did not exist in written form. Instead, for untold numbers of centuries they passed from one generation to another orally, or by word of mouth. Only in the late medieval period did British writers such as the twelfth-century teacher and bishop Geoffrey of Monmouth commit such stories to paper.

Geoffrey and others like him did a great service to later generations. Because they lived and worked so long ago, however, it is often difficult to know how much of their writings came from the old oral tales. According to British historian Richard Barber, "Geoffrey did not have an ordered set of written chronicles on which to draw. Our problem today is to know how much was due to his imagination, and how much to the old traditions handed down by bards [storytellers], highly trained in the art of memory, but also skilled in rhetoric [public speaking] and poetry."[2]

Indeed, at first and for a very long time the survival of the ancient British myths and legends relied on their memorization and recitation by the bards. Typically, they told the tales either around a campfire or hearth following the evening meal or in a larger public gathering in the daytime. Such a bard, who made his living that way, traveled from town to town and received donations from the local citizens in exchange for entertaining them.

It is important to understand that such repeated oral tellings of myths were not identical, nor even nearly so, in structure and vocabulary. As Gettysburg College scholar Christopher R. Fee points out:

> Oral storytellers work in ways fundamentally different from their literate counterparts. While a written story—once committed to paper—remains static [unchanged] through multiple readings, oral storytellers did not ply their craft through rote repetition of the same stories. Instead, working from a bare outline of characters and events committed to memory, a storyteller wove a new narrative in each retelling of any particular story. The general players and conflicts remained the same, to be sure, but the storyteller also drew upon a huge hoard [collection] of stock characterizations and associations, mythic elements, poetic metaphors, and the like. . . . All this material . . . shifted from telling to telling, as the poet strove to emphasize different points.[3]

Eventually, such mythic storytellers became increasingly scarce, as the need for their profession waned. The main reason was the steady rise of literacy and writing among the general populace and the creation and growing availability of printed books. Scholar Richard Jones explains:

> Over a period of several hundred years, the art of storytelling moved from the spoken to the written word as authors, historians, poets, and playwrights began

condensing a wide variety of often contradictory traditions into one *definitive* [authoritative or classic] version. . . . And so it has continued down through the ages. By the 18th and 19th centuries, most of the well-known myths and legends—such as those of King Arthur, Robin Hood, and Lady Godiva—had arrived at the form in which they would be handed down to us. [Since that time] the basic characters and narratives have remained static.[4]

Quest for an Acceptable Ancestry

During the many centuries before the old myths were committed to paper and set in stone, so to speak, little by little the inhabitants of Britain left their marks on them. People could relate to these stories in part because the characters, settings, and situations closely reflected their own particular customs, beliefs, and experiences. After all, part of the bard's job was to make the tales he told appealing to his listeners. Thus, in Fee's words, "The myths and legends of any people have much to tell us about the nature of that people, and the early British cultures are revealed to us, in some small part, as much by the types of stories they told and the way that they told them as by what any given story was about."[5]

A number of the surviving ancient British myths reveal that the medieval British wanted to appear to be as cultured and sophisticated as the French, Italians, and other peoples who lived in continental Europe. Centuries earlier, when Britain had been part of the Roman Empire, the isles and their inhabitants had been seen as dwelling on the semi-barbaric fringes of the civilized Roman world. Even worse, in the 400s the Roman government, whose dominion was then slowly but steadily collapsing, pulled its troops out of Britain. Roman Britons found themselves in a very real sense abandoned even as they were under attack by Germanic tribes.

After Rome's disintegration in the fifth and sixth centuries, therefore, early medieval times witnessed British culture developing largely on a separate track from continental European society. Eventually, some of the few Britons who were literate at the time wanted to establish the worth of their own ancestry. Their quest was to show that their cultural heritage was every bit as good and acceptable as those of the Italians and other Europeans who lived closer to the heart of the defunct Roman realm. They did this by creating myths about the origins of British culture.

Brutus Is Born

Geoffrey of Monmouth was one of these educated British. He knew that the great ancient Roman writer Virgil had claimed in his epic, the *Aeneid*, that the Romans had descended from Aeneas, a prince of Troy, the ancient city sacked by the Greeks during the famous Trojan War. It was widely assumed that Aeneas and his Roman descendants had carried on the heroic and noble traditions of the brave warriors who had fought at Troy. So the obvious way for the medieval British to build up their cultural image was to establish their own connection to the Trojan War.

That elusive connection was supplied by a series of myths about an ancient figure named Brutus. He was said to be both Aeneas's great grandson and the founder and first king of Britain. As Ashe tells it:

> Some unknown readers of Virgil, impressed by what he said about the Trojan ancestry of the Romans, had the notion of taking the story further and giving the Britons the same honorable origin. [The Welsh, Cornish, and several other early residents of Britain had already] preserved vague traditions of a glorious unity in the past. One of Geoffrey's main purposes was to substantiate these traditions with a splendid national history. He picked up the Brutus tale as an excellent beginning.[6]

The first written source that mentions Brutus's myth was the *Historia Britonum* ("History of the Britons"), a ninth-century historical tract by a Welsh monk named Nennius. However, Geoffrey of Monmouth's later work, the *Historia Regum Britanniae* ("History of the Kings of Britain"), contains a longer and more often-cited version of the story. According to Geoffrey, Brutus, a descendant of the Trojan

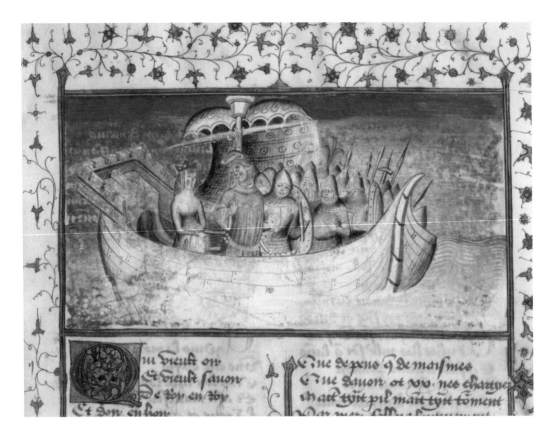

A fifteenth-century illustrated page from Geoffrey of Monmouth's History of the Kings of Britain *depicts Brutus setting sail to found Britain.*

hero Aeneas, wandered through various lands until he came to a deserted island. There, he had a dream in which a goddess told him how to reach a large island on which he was destined to settle.

On the way to his destiny, Brutus got into a war with the locals in Gaul (now France) before finally arriving on the large island the goddess had spoken of. Barber picks up the story there, saying:

> At the time the island was called Albion, and was only inhabited by a few giants. The pleasant aspect of the land, the abundance of fish in its rivers and deer in its forests, filled Brutus and his companions with the desire to settle there. So, after exploring part of the land, they drove the giants they found there to take refuge in mountain caves, and divided the country among them by casting lots [choosing by random drawing]. [The newcomers] began to till the fields

and build houses, so that in a little while you might have thought it had been inhabited from time immemorial. Then Brutus called the island Britain, and his companions Britons, after his own name, in order to perpetuate his memory.[7]

The Power of Myths

Brutus then proceeded to establish a city—"New Troy," which in future ages would come to be called London. When he died, Britain was divided between his three sons. Locrinus ruled England, while Albanactus became king of Scotland, and their brother Kamber took charge of Wales. The ultimate legacy of these early kings was that later English historians all began their works with Brutus's tale. Indeed, as late as 1600, the myths surrounding him and his sons were widely considered to be true.

As a result, a large stone said to mark the spot where Brutus and his party first landed in Britain is still a popular tourist attraction. (It is located in the town of Totnes, in southwestern England.) Moreover, although historians have determined that Brutus's tale was only a legend, the people who live in the region regularly retell it as part of their proud cultural heritage.

In a similar manner the huge number of British myths, representing the combined legendary tales of several ancient and medieval peoples, remain a vital part of Britain's overall cultural heritage. Furthermore, those colorful traditions are known and admired worldwide. Characters such as King Leir, King Arthur, and Robin Hood, whose stories began in simple, local word-of-mouth versions, are now complex, universal icons who continue to inspire retellings in print, as well as on film. Such is the power of beloved myths—to live on and on by enchanting each new generation.

CHAPTER 1

Myths Born of a Clash of Cultures

It is impossible to appreciate the cultural significance of Britain's great melting pot of myths without a grasp of the diverse and often dissimilar peoples that came together to form the British nation. Among others they included the Celts (most often pronounced KELTS), Romans, Anglo-Saxons, and Norse (or Vikings). Their divergent cultures clashed at first, causing enormous amounts of distrust, violence, and death. But over time they steadily united and in the process absorbed one another's customs, gods, beliefs, and frequently their myths.

These events produced what Christopher R. Fee calls a "vibrant confluence of mythic influences." He colorfully adds, "In the medieval literary traditions of Britain, the voices of the gods of the Celts, Romans, Saxons, and Vikings combine in a chorus that can seem chaotic and confused, but one that also offers us a rich and distinctly British melody."[8] A brief examination of these cultures and how they arrived in Britain reveals how this cultural assimilation took place and produced the splendid, incredibly varied collection of British myths.

The Earliest Britons

The original natives of Britain were what people today most often call "cave dwellers" or "prehistoric humans." Primitive hunter-gatherers who moved from place to place following herds of animals, they inhabited what is now England at least as early as five hundred thousand years ago. Almost nothing is known about their society. What is more certain is that their world changed in a major way roughly ten thousand years ago (around 8000 B.C.). Before that time, what are now the British Isles made up a single landmass connected to mainland Europe by a narrow bridge of low-lying swampland. In about 8000 B.C. sea levels rose, causing that bridge to disappear and making Britain an island. Roughly two millennia later (c. 6000 B.C.), Ireland separated from the rest of Britain, creating a second large island.

Another major turning point for the inhabitants of those islands came in about 4500 B.C. The nomadic locals settled down and began practicing agriculture and raising livestock. They formed tribal groups in various local regions and came to be ruled by local chieftains.

An archeological reconstruction shows a prehistoric village in Britain. By 4500 B.C., Britons had begun practicing agriculture and animal husbandry and lived in villages of thatched huts.

These original Britons almost certainly shared cultural similarities. They lived in small huts made of wood, thatch, and other perishable materials and used stone or bone tools and weapons. Around 2200 B.C. they learned to make copper versions of these implements and over time mastered gold and silver smelting and making bronze (an alloy of copper and tin) as well. Their religious beliefs and myths are largely unknown. Some experts think that, like some other prehistoric Europeans, they may have considered certain animals to be sacred and/or prayed to nature spirits or the spirits of ancestors.

Coming of the Celts

Much of this changed in a big way when in the early to mid-first millennium (1000s) B.C. succeeding waves of Celts from northern Europe entered Britain. Among the more important of Europe's early peoples, the Celts occupied most of the northern portions of the European continent and the

Gods Like Human Heroes

Unlike the Greeks and Romans, the Celts often pictured their gods as their own distant ancestors rather than as their creators. This made these deities in large degree interchangeable with human heroes. Historian Peter Berresford Ellis elaborates:

The Celts made their heroes into gods and their gods into heroes. In the lives of these gods and heroes, the lives of the people and the essence of their religious traditions were mirrored. Celtic heroes . . . were totally human and were subject to all the natural virtues and vices. . . . Yet their world was one of rural happiness, a world in which they indulged in all the pleasures of mortal life in an idealized form: love of nature, art, games, feasting, hunting, and heroic single-handed combat.

Peter Berresford Ellis. *The Celtic Empire: The First Millennium of Celtic History, c.1000 B.C.– A.D. 51.* Durham, NC: Carolina Academic Press, 1990, pp. 16–17.

British Isles between roughly 1200 and 100 B.C. During these centuries they came into periodic contact with the Greeks and Romans who lived in and dominated southern Europe.

The Celts, whom the Greeks called *Keltoi* (KEL-tee) and the Romans *Celtae* (KEL-tie), possessed neither cities nor writing and were mostly rural farmers and animal herders. For this reason the Greco-Roman world mistakenly saw them as barbarians. The reality was that the Celts knew metallurgy (the science of metals) and had laws, complex social organization, and well-developed religious beliefs and myths, making them no less civilized than the Romans.

Because the Celts were illiterate, their beliefs and myths passed from generation to generation orally. Based on later descriptions by Greco-Roman writers and Christian monks, Celtic religion worshipped many gods, like that of the Greeks and Romans. A major difference was that many of the Celtic deities began as more or less formless nature spirits. They did not begin to take human form until after the Celts had experienced prolonged contact with the Romans and their human-like gods. Because Celtic peoples spread across numerous lands over the course of many centuries, individual tribes and other groups often had their own local gods. In Celtic Ireland, for example, Angus Mac Og was the god of youth and love, and Brigit (or Brigid) was the goddess of crafts, healing, and prophecy. In Scotland, by comparison, the goddess of prophecy was Corra. In Wales, meanwhile, Arawn was god of the dead and the Underworld, and Dylan was the sea god. There were also a large number of "pan-Celtic" deities, that is, gods who were recognized throughout most or all of the European Celtic lands. Cernunnos, the lord of animals, a deity sporting a set of antlers, was such a pan-Celtic divinity. So was Lugh, a sun god and master of the arts, including music; Morrigan (or Morrigu), a fierce war goddess; and Epona, divine mistress of horses. Modern scholars think there may have been close to two hundred Celtic deities in all.

Standing between this mighty array of gods and average worshippers were the Druids, the priests of Celtic religion. According to the famous Roman general Julius Caesar, who encountered several Celtic tribes during his conquest of Gaul

The *Mabinogion*

Many of the medieval Welsh myths come from a collection of writings known as the *Four Branches of the Mabinogi,* sometimes called the *Mabinogion.* Modern estimates for when the tales it contains originated range from about A.D. 1060 to 1200.

in the 50s B.C., the Druids performed regular sacrifices to the gods. Some of these were human sacrifices, he said, adding, "The Druids are exempt from military service and do not pay taxes like the rest [of the Gauls]. . . . They lay particular stress on their belief that the soul does not perish, but passes after death from one body to another, and they consider that this belief is the best possible encouragement to courage, since it does away with the fear of death."[9]

Celtic Society and Customs

The fact that the Druids did not have to fight in battle or pay taxes shows clearly that they were very highly regarded in Celtic society. Indeed, some evidence suggests that they had a number of other important tasks and roles beside those related to religious worship. Druids acted as judges in legal disputes, for example, and kept local calendars and explained how they worked to average folk. In addition, it appears that the Druids acted as teachers. They also were society's scholars, so to speak. Although the original Celts had little in the way of written languages, they had much in the way of folklore and social history, which the Druids preserved mostly by committing it to memory.

The Druids belonged to one of the three main classes in Celtic society. The highest class was made up of the king and his leading warriors, who formed the Celtic version of nobility. These people seem to have dwelled mainly in large hill forts, which the Romans called *oppida.* Remnants of more than three thousand of them have been found in Britain alone. A typical *oppidum* was built from large stones and masses of packed earth, reinforced by long, stout pieces of timber.

The second class in Celtic society, which was evidently almost equal in status to the first, was composed of the Druids and any poets or thinkers who may have existed in one tribe or another. The third class was made up of all the other people in society—the common folk, so to speak. Thus, the members of the first two classes represented a very small minority of the population.

Like the Romans and other European peoples, the Celts made their livings primarily through agriculture. However, they also carried on vigorous trade, not only with other Celtic groups, but also with the Romans and Greeks who lived to the south of the Celtic lands. In exchange for various luxury items from the Greco-Roman world, the Celts traded raw metals such as iron, gold, silver, and lead, which they mined. Celtic artisans were very adept at fashioning these metals into bracelets, pendants, rings, earrings, goblets, axes, and swords, which they also traded.

Druids, the priests of the Celts, acted as judges, teachers, and calendar keepers and were exempt from paying taxes and doing military service.

Excavating a Celtic Hill Fort

A Celtic hill fort on Burrough Hill in Leicestershire, in central England, has long been known to archaeologists. But only minor excavations took place there before 2010, when diggers from the University of Leicester began investigating it. A spokesperson for the university provides the following facts about the fort, which flourished between about 600 B.C. and the A.D. 40s:

Situated on major routes and strategically positioned among neighboring hill forts, Burrough Hill was clearly an important settlement for many years. . . . Some authorities believe that it may have been the capital of the Coritani, a collection of tribes who ruled the East Midlands during the 1st century AD. The Coritani were an agricultural people and were on good terms with the occupying Romans, who offered a degree of protection against warlike neighboring tribes. One of the fort's most impressive elements, which the University of Leicester archaeologists have been examining, is the remains of a gatehouse, complete with cobbled road. The current survey has also revealed that the settlement extended much further east than previously believed, with the remains of numerous roundhouses and grain pits now identified.

Mike Simpson. "Excavations and Open Day at Iron Age Hill Fort." *Newsblog*, University of Leicester, June 18, 2010. www2.le.ac.uk/news/blog/2010-archive/june-2010/excavations-and-open-day-at-iron-age-hillfort.

An ancient Celtic hill fort is seen here from the air. Excavations on such forts have only just begun.

The Celts lived mostly in northern Europe, where winters were longer and colder than in the lands along the Mediterranean Sea. So they rarely wore tunics that left their legs bare, as did the Greeks and Romans, who dwelled in those warmer lands. Instead, typical Celtic male attire consisted of wool or linen long-sleeved shirts and trousers that went down to the ankles. In the coldest months they wore a woolen cape over these garments. Women also wore capes over their own standard clothing, which consisted of a body-length dress, sometimes cinched in the middle by a belt.

The Celts were also known for their bravery and prowess in war. Warriors wielded long metal swords and often conducted wild, screaming charges at the enemy. To increase the frightening effect of such a tactic, sometimes the warriors stripped down and fought naked. The first time that a Roman army encountered such an attack by naked, boisterous warriors, the mostly inexperienced recruits in the Roman ranks simply turned and ran for their lives! (Subsequent improvements in Rome's military made it much more disciplined and effective and more than a match for the average Celtic army.)

The Religiously Tolerant Romans

With their improved and much respected and feared army, the Romans launched a series of invasions of Celtic-controlled Britain in the first century A.D. The armies of Rome were victorious. For nearly four centuries after that, what is now England was a Roman province, where Roman cities, temples, baths, and roads were built and Roman laws and armies prevailed. However, the Romans were never able to decisively conquer all of Scotland and Wales, which remained largely Celtic enclaves.

Most of the Celts in England, however, had to follow Roman laws and adapt at least somewhat to Roman social customs. The biggest changes were experienced by Celts who dwelled in the towns. For the most part, the Celts had no towns, but rather lived in small, unstructured villages with dirt paths and huts made of perishable materials. In contrast, Roman urban life was highly structured. It featured paved roads set up in grid patterns and extensive use of large, stone public buildings, including law courts, religious temples, public baths, and amphitheaters for public spectacles. For average Celts, who bathed only rarely, the Roman custom of attending the baths daily at first must have seemed extremely strange.

The Romans also brought with them their myths of daring and gallant Roman heroes of the past, including the Trojan prince Aeneas, celebrated as the founder of the Roman race. They also introduced their gods and myths, which were largely Romanized versions of older Greek gods and myths. Thus, the Roman Jupiter was the equivalent of the Greek Zeus, and the myths originally associated with Zeus carried over to the religious lore surrounding Jupiter.

In addition, the highly religiously tolerant Romans allowed most Celtic worship and myth telling to go on as before. Moreover, the Romans came to respect a number of Celtic gods and welcomed them into their own pantheon. The result was the worship of several Romano-Celtic deities, including a war goddess, Andraste; Aveta, goddess of birth and midwifery; Britannia, who was associated with Minerva, Roman goddess of war and wisdom; and a god of healing, Ocelus.

The Anglo-Saxon Invasions

As the Celts had, the Romans ultimately lost control of Britain. When the western Roman realm fell to marauding Germanic tribes in the fifth and sixth centuries, some of those same tribes crossed the English Channel and invaded Britain. Chief among these intruders were the Angles, Saxons, Jutes, and Frisians. Most were absorbed over time by the first two groups; hence the later common term *Anglo-Saxon* to describe the dominant residents of Britain between about 550 and 1066. The Anglo-Saxons established several small but fiercely independent kingdoms in what is now England, including Mercia, Northumbria, East Anglia, Sussex, and Wessex (with its capital of London).

The invaders also introduced a religious tradition that featured a rich array of gods and myths. Many of these gods were somewhat altered versions of Norse (Viking) deities. This is because the Angles, Saxons, and Norse were all of Germanic stock and therefore shared a number of customs

Celtic Human Sacrifice

The famous Roman politician and military general Julius Caesar, who described his exploits in Gaul (now France) in considerable detail, said the following about the practice of human sacrifice among the Celts who dwelled there. Modern historians think the British Celts likely had a similar practice.

The Gauls [are] extremely superstitious. As a result, people who are seriously ill or who have to face the dangers of battle will either make or promise to make human sacrifices, employing the Druids [priests] as officiating ministers at these rites. They believe that the divine majesty can only be appeased if one human life is offered in exchange for another, and they have sacrifices of this kind established as a regular state [government] institution. . . . They believe that the gods prefer the execution of men who have been caught in the act of theft or armed robbery or some other crime.

Julius Caesar. *Commentaries.* Published as *War Commentaries of Caesar.* Translated by Rex Warner. New York: Plume, 1987, p. 124.

Roman soldiers rush to stop Druids from making a human sacrifice at Stonehenge in this drawing.

and beliefs inherited from a common ancestral group. The chief god of the Anglo-Saxons, Woden, for instance, was a close counterpart of the leading Norse deity Odin. Both gods oversaw warriors engaged in battle. Similarly, Thunor, the Anglo-Saxon god of the sky and thunder, was a version of the Norse thunder god Thor; and Frey (or Freo), goddess of love and fertility for the Anglo-Saxons, was equivalent to Freya, who held those same attributes for the Norse.

Attack of the Norsemen

The Anglo-Saxons' dominance in Britain did not go unchallenged. Beginning in 793 or 794, several Norse groups assaulted the British Isles. In June of that year, St. Cuthbert's, a widely revered and wealthy church situated on the tiny island of Lindisfarne, off Britain's eastern coast, was overrun by Viking raiders.

By this time Christian churches were common across England and the rest of the British Isles. Christianity had originally been introduced to the region by the Romans, mainly in the fourth century, when that faith was rising to prominence in Rome. (Late in that century, it became Rome's

Viking raiders land in Britain. The Vikings plundered ancient Britain for two centuries before Alfred the Great defeated them.

official faith, replacing the long-lived polytheistic group of gods headed by Jupiter.) In the fifth century, however, Rome, then under attack by numerous northern European tribes, abandoned Britain. Although a few people in England remained Christian, over time the old Celtic beliefs regained popularity and eventually dominance in the region, especially after the influx of pagan Anglo-Saxons, who still worshipped the Celtic deities.

Another major religious transition occurred after Rome's fall in the late 400s. In the three centuries that followed, representatives of the Christian churches in Italy went out and converted many of the Celtic and Germanic peoples who had brought Rome down. Some of these missionaries went to the British Isles and converted the natives, so by the time the Viking invasions started in the late 700s, most of the people in the region followed Christian beliefs, and Christian churches dotted the landscape.

The Vikings, who at this time had not yet been exposed to Christianity, looted the church on Lindisfarne and the nearby buildings and slaughtered most of the monks. These terrifying acts prompted Alcuin, a Christian scholar who lived in the English town of York, to write, "Never before has such terror appeared in Britain, as we have now suffered from a pagan race. Nor was it thought possible that such an inroad from the sea could be made. Behold the Church of St. Cuthbert, spattered with the blood of the priests of God, despoiled of all its ornaments. A place more venerable than any other in Britain has fallen prey to pagans."[10]

In the next two centuries, Norse raiding parties attacked British and Irish towns far and wide. Some of the invaders eventually settled on British soil. In 866 a huge Viking army marched westward from Britain's eastern coast and defeated the forces of several of the Anglo-Saxon kingdoms. Finally, only Wessex, ruled by Alfred, was left. He and his supporters fled into some impenetrable marshes. There they erected a

Boudica's Uprising

During the insurrection led by the Celtic leader Boudica in A.D. 60 to 61, the rebels sacked three of the largest towns in Britain—Camulodunum (modern-day Colchester), Londinium (London), and Verulamium (St. Albans). An estimated seventy thousand to eighty thousand people were killed in the uprising before the Romans rebounded and defeated Boudica.

Sources for Norse Myths

Many of the Norse/Anglo-Saxon gods and myths are mentioned in two important late medieval northern European documents—the *Poetic Edda* and the *Prose Edda*, both dating from the 1200s. The *Prose Edda* was written by a talented Icelandic poet, politician, and historian named Snorri Sturluson (1179–1241).

fortress, which became their base camp for counterattacks on the enemy. These were largely successful. Alfred was finally able to defeat the intruders decisively, after which he concluded a treaty with them.

The treaty provided for the Vikings' exit from Wessex. In the years that followed, the Vikings created the Danelaw, a wide Norse occupation zone that stretched across eastern England. The native Anglo-Saxons were not happy having the enemy in their very midst, however. So Alfred's successors, aided by other English leaders, steadily drove the Norse out of the Danelaw. By the 950s the Viking settlements were gone, yet some individual Norse settlers remained and mingled with the locals. They, along with the long Viking occupation, added a new layer of customs, religion, and myths to the British melting pot. The fact that the mythologies of the Anglo-Saxons and Norse were so similar has made it difficult for modern scholars. They are often unsure whether it was the native Anglo-Saxons or the Viking immigrants that had more influence on the surviving myths about Woden, Thunor, and other deities in that pantheon.

The Norman Conquest

The myths of the Anglo-Saxons and Norse eventually faded in importance in Britain. This was because of the continuing powerful influence of Christianity. From the 700s through the 900s, that faith steadily grew stronger and more influential in England. But the event that dealt the biggest blow of all to the older religions and assured the triumph of Christian beliefs among the lower classes was the Norman invasion of Britain in 1066. The Normans, who hailed from northwestern France, were a mixture of French and Viking cultures. They were also devout Christians. Under their leader, William the Conqueror, they crossed the English Channel and in the

Battle of Hastings defeated an army led by the Anglo-Saxon ruler Harold.

In the years that followed, William reorganized the local government and military and erected numerous castles across the land. He also forever changed the nature of large-scale religion, worship, and mythologizing in Britain. As a researcher for Britain's biggest modern media outlet, the BBC, puts it:

> It was the Norman Conquest that really cemented the power of the church in England. William the Conqueror implemented a colossal building project at both monastic and parish level. In Winchester, for example, the old Saxon Minster made way for a new Norman building. These new stone churches continued to play a central role in community life. They acted as schools, market places and entertainment venues. The medieval period in Britain is really a story of how Christianity came to dominate the lives of the ordinary people, both at home and on the long and perilous journeys of pilgrimage.[11]

A scene from the Bayeux Tapestry depicts the death of King Harold at the Battle of Hastings in 1066. The Norman Conquest resulted in a transformation of British society.

The subsequent complex blending of Norman, Anglo-Saxon, Norse, and Celtic heritages, along with the Christian faith, began to lay the foundations for the modern English nation. The pagan myths at first remained. But the stories in the Christian Bible about the creation, the ancient Hebrews and their prophets, and Jesus and his apostles steadily came to overshadow the older myths, some of which disappeared forever. New British myths took their place in late medieval times. Most of these dealt with the exploits of characters, who were all Christians and who were either real or possibly real. Among them were the Scottish hero William Wallace, the Saxon noblewoman Lady Godiva, and the English outlaw Robin Hood.

Yet these tales about early Christianity and/or heroes who worshipped the Christian god did not negate or completely

After his conquest William reorganized local government and the military and built numerous castles, including Rochester Castle (shown), throughout Britain to solidify his rule.

erase the wonderfully rich pagan mythical traditions. A fair number of the pre-Christian myths managed to survive to the present day and will likely continue to endure for a long time to come. In Fee's words, "Although Christianity undoubtedly carried the day in Britain, all of the mythologies of Britain were transformed through their contact with one another, and the literary tradition of medieval Britain is a testament to the long-term influence of early pagan narrative traditions upon later Christian Britain."[12]

CHAPTER 2

Tales of the Ancient British Gods

S ome of the most famous, quaint, and interesting tales from the corpus of surviving British myths are those that deal with the exploits of the gods revered by the various peoples who settled in ancient and medieval Britain. Some of these tales are long and fairly detailed. Others are short, fragmentary, and/or hard to understand and interpret.

A major reason for this wide variation in the length and quality of the surviving myths, including those about the gods, is the often chaotic nature of the societies in which the myth tellers worked. As new invaders and settlers frequently arrived and took charge, they absorbed existing native myths in a hap-hazard manner. Some tales were downgraded in importance and preserved in abbreviated form, while an unknown number of others were lost altogether. About the diverse groups of surviving British deities, Christopher R. Fee writes:

> The often violent confrontations and destructions or assimilations of ethnic groups and their religions— Celtic and Roman, Romano-Celtic and Germanic, [and so forth] . . . renders clear [descriptions of many gods] difficult to isolate. Furthermore, the lack of written records left by cultures that tended to transmit information orally leads almost inevitably to a coloring [and alteration] of earlier [gods] by more literate

peoples. . . . Both the Germanic and Celtic pantheons were reworked to varying degrees by Christian monks anxious to uphold Christianity [and] so it was that gods and goddesses of ancient Germanic, and especially Celtic, pantheons were either destroyed or demoted if they could not be assimilated or converted in some way to the new religion.[13]

The Mysterious Green Man

The so-called Green Man was an ancient Celtic fertility god more specifically named Herne. Modern experts think that in prehistoric Celtic worship of this horned deity, the priest or shaman dressed in a deerskin and wore a deer mask complete with horns. In the twentieth century evidence emerged suggesting that the original ancient town that stood where London does now was central to the Green Man cult. First, it has been suggested that Herne Hill in south London was named for that god and may have been where early worshippers met. A number of scholars point out that some other places in London may be named after various aspects of the mysterious Green Man. Also, certain time-honored agricultural festivals associated with worship of that god continued to be practiced in the London area right into the twentieth century. Among them were several May Day and May Pole observances in which worshippers danced and feasted in honor of the Green Man. This shows that at least a few Celtic religious customs never completely died out, despite the suppression and replacement of the Celtic faith by Christianity.

Dancing around the May Pole is a festivity with roots in ancient Celtic religion.

In whatever form the myths of the British gods have survived, all of these stories agree on one point—that the world in which those deities dwelled was one of jarring yet vivid extremes. On the one hand, strife was frequent, as the deities often battled both monsters and humans. On the other, that world was also one of great tranquility and beauty. During peaceful times the human-like gods wandered through rolling, wooded hills and green, fragrant valleys interlaced with the purest of sparkling streams.

Gods as Human Ancestors

The Welsh Celts contributed many popular myths to British culture. Many of those surviving Welsh and other British Celtic myths picture the gods as kings, queens, princesses, and other flesh-and-blood characters engaging in marriages, wars, captivity, suffering, and other human-like activities. Modern scholars think that this was partly because of the unique nature of ancient Celtic beliefs about the gods. As a noted authority on the Celts, Peter Berresford Ellis, points out, "The deities of Celtic myth tend to be the ancestors of the people rather than their creators. . . . They are all totally human and subject to all the natural virtues and vices. No sin is exempt from practice by the gods or humans."[14]

In addition to having human form, habits, and weaknesses, most of the Celtic gods were mortal rather than eternal, as the gods of most other ancient peoples were thought to be. In other words, although the Celtic deities aged very slowly and usually lived much longer than the average human, eventually they died; they could also be killed or die by accident. That in itself was a highly unusual trait for so-called gods. Once dead, however, they changed into another form, frequently some sort of spirit. So even though they were not physically immortal, they *were* spiritually eternal.

Regardless of their human form and very human failings, these deities did typically have certain superhuman attributes such as abnormally great strength, size, speed, or wisdom. Moreover, some of them were highly skilled in the arts, sciences, conjuring magic spells, and composing poetry. So although they had limitations and flaws, the gods also possessed numerous extraordinary qualities that people tended to respect and admire greatly. So for most Celts, worship of these deities consisted primarily of rituals meant to express that respect and admiration.

The exact nature of most of those rituals is not known, but experts think they included initiation ceremonies; sacrificing animals and using parts of their bodies to predict the future; feasting in honor of the gods; and conducting healing rites, such as immersing one's body in "sacred" water. There were also requests made to the deities through prayer—most often asking either that a god bestow a blessing on oneself or a friend, or conversely, that a deity do harm to one's enemy.

The distinctly human attributes of most Celtic gods were further heightened by the Christian monks who later committed these tales to paper. To most of these monks, of course, the Celtic gods were not real, or at least not divine. Moreover, a number of educated Christians came to believe

A panel of The Gundestrup Cauldron, thought to be a first-century B.C. depiction of a Celtic god. It shows themes of both animal and human sacrifice.

that if those deities *were* real, they were some kind of evil spirits. So in their versions of the myths, the monks robbed the gods of most of their superhuman status and depicted them largely as ordinary people. The writers did keep in a few superhuman and/or supernatural elements they deemed harmless—just enough to ensure that the stories were still entertaining.

The Tragedy of Branwen and Bran

This was certainly the case in one of the most popular of these ancient tales—the tragic story of the goddess Branwen and her brother Bendigeidfran, more commonly called "Bran the Blessed" or just "Bran." In the surviving version of the myth, Bran is a giant, just as he was in the original Celtic version. Another supernatural element retained by the Christian monks is a severed head that can still think and speak.

Long ago, the tale opens, the kingdoms of Wales and Ireland were frequently at odds, and their differences sometimes led to war. For that reason, many people on both sides were relieved to hear that a powerful Irish ruler, King Matholwch, planned to marry Branwen, daughter of the Welsh sea god Llyr. The union seemed to promise a new era of peace between the two lands. Branwen's brother Bran was among those who had high hopes for the marriage.

However, Branwen's other brother, the mean-spirited and antisocial Efnisien, strongly objected to the marriage. To emphasize his displeasure, in Ellis's words he secretly "slunk into the camp of Matholwch in disguise and proceeded to cut off the tails, ears, eyebrows, and lips"[15] of the king's horses. Then he fled in great haste. The enraged Matholwch hurried to Bran and demanded an explanation. After telling Matholwch that the disgruntled Efnisien had done the awful deed, Bran tried to make amends by giving the Irish king new horses, as well as a magical cauldron having the power to bring fallen warriors back to life.

Matholwch accepted these gifts and for a while following the wedding appeared to be satisfied. But deep down he was still boiling mad about the loss of his beloved horses, so he decided to vent his anger on his new bride. "He had her removed to the kitchens of the palace," Ellis writes, "and forced her to cook and clean and ordered the chief cook to give her a blow on the ears every day so that she would know her place. All traffic of ships between [Ireland] and [Wales] was forbidden, so that no news of how Branwen was being punished should reach her brother [Bran]."[16]

But Matholwch's wicked scheme was foiled by the victim herself. Branwen secretly trained a starling to carry a message to Bran, who after reading it immediately amassed an army for the invasion of Ireland. According to Geoffrey Ashe, "The army sailed across the sea, but the giant Bran waded [across]. . . . The Irish king's [lookouts] were the first to sight the Britons. They told him a mountain and a forest were approaching over the water. The mountain was Bran, [and] the trees were the masts of his ships."[17]

Bran and his forces won the ensuing battle. However, during the fighting Bran was wounded by a poisoned spear and it became clear that he would soon die. To everyone's surprise, he ordered his men to cut off his head and take it home. There, he said, it should be buried and would thereafter act as a magic charm to help repel invaders. The soldiers carried out the order to decapitate Bran, but they were shocked when right afterward his eyes moved and he continued to speak to them, giving them further orders and telling them stories. When at last the head went silent and was buried, Bran's saddened sister Branwen died of a broken heart.

A Human Bridge

In the tale of Branwen and Bran, when Matholwch learned that the enemy was approaching from the sea, he ordered the local river bridges destroyed, hoping to make it difficult for Bran and his army to reach the Irish towns. But the huge Bran laid down, transforming his body into a bridge, over which his soldiers marched on the Irish.

What the Myth Reveals

For archaeologists and other modern scholars who study the Celtic societies of Wales and Ireland, the ancient myth of Branwen and Bran is revealing in several ways. First, it suggests that the two lands had social contact with each other in pre-Roman times. This has been confirmed by archaeology, which shows that the ancient Irish and Welsh traded with each other and sometimes planted colonies on each other's

Magic cauldrons featured prominently in Celtic religion. In the legend of Bran and Branwen, such a cauldron was used to bring dead warriors back to life.

soil. Experts think it is plausible that the war described in the myth is a cultural memory of tensions and violence caused by those colonies.

The myth of Branwen and Bran also reflects some ancient Celtic religious beliefs. Even after his body dies, for instance, Bran's head remains alive and speaks to his soldiers, indicating that his spirit lives on after his body dies. This is exactly how most ancient Celts viewed death. They felt that a person's spirit, or soul, survived the body's demise by being reborn in the afterlife, which they called the Otherworld. Moreover, when the soul aged and eventually died in the Otherworld, it was reborn again in the human world and the cycle kept on repeating. This preoccupation with the concept of rebirth was also reflected in another detail of the story—the magic cauldron that could bring dead warriors back to life.

In addition, the myth preserves other ancient Celtic religious and cultural beliefs and customs, most prominently those involving human heads. As Ellis explains:

> It is important to remember that, for the ancient Celts, the soul reposed in the head. . . . [They] would take and keep the heads of those people they respected, embalming them with cedar oil, and thus paying reverence to great souls. They were not, as some have claimed, head *hunters*. Only the heads of those already slain in battle, friend or foe, were taken as trophies, and always people worthy of respect. Sometimes the heads were placed in sanctuaries [safe areas protected by religious authorities] or, more often, were placed in the sacred Celtic rivers as . . . offerings [to the gods].[18]

Roman and Celtic Gods Interact

The Celtic practice of venerating selected human heads was one of many unfamiliar native customs the Romans encountered when they seized control of what is now England in the first century. It has been established that, in their usual way, the Romans tolerated native religious traditions. Thus, worship of most of the old Celtic gods continued, as did the perpetuation of the Celtic myths.

Nevertheless, both the Romans and native Celts were fascinated by each other's gods and myths. Over time some of their deities and mythical tales began to interact in various ways. "This interaction," scholar Miranda J. Green points out, "resulted in wide-scale representation of the [Celtic] gods [in Roman statues, literary descriptions, and so forth], many of whom were totally alien to the Greco-Roman pantheon."[19] Thanks to these physical depictions, some of which have been found by archaeologists, the identities of a number of old Celtic gods that otherwise might have been lost over the centuries survived.

Most of the myths of these Romano-Celtic gods have not survived. One of the exceptions is a story about the bloodthirsty Andraste, who before the Roman invasion was associated with the Iceni, a Celtic tribe inhabiting eastern England. In A.D. 60 Boudica, queen of the Iceni, decided to rebel against the Romans. Before launching her initial attack, she addressed her troops and gave them the impression that their war goddess, Andraste, was standing in their midst. According to the Roman historian Dio Cassius, when Boudica paused in her speech,

> a hare escaped from the fold of her dress. And since it ran on what they considered the auspicious [favorable] side, the whole multitude shouted with pleasure, and [Boudica], raising her hand toward heaven, said: "I thank you, Andraste, and call upon you as woman speaking to woman. . . . I supplicate [beg] and pray [to you] for victory, preservation of life, and liberty against [the] insolent, unjust, insatiable, impious [Romans].[20]

The soldiers "shouted with pleasure" because they believed that Andraste herself had directed the hare to move in a promising manner. Moreover, they and other Celts believed that the goddess remained with them as they proceeded to assault and sack two Roman cities. Those Romans who were taken prisoner were taken to Andraste's sacred grove of trees and there slaughtered as a sacrifice to her. The myth of Andraste's wrath against the Romans continued to inspire the Iceni and other Celts for some time to come. These events demonstrate how strong religious beliefs can, during the tensions and stress of wartime, give rise to new myths that are then perpetuated among fellow believers. (The Romans eventually defeated Boudica, after which she either poisoned herself or died of illness.)

The interaction of Roman and Celtic religious ideas and gods also produced several Romano-Celtic deities. In some cases, like that of the war goddess Andraste, to whom Queen

Boudica prayed, they were hybrid gods that did not exist in either pantheon. In other cases, by contrast, a deity in one pantheon was associated with, or thought to be equivalent to, a god in the other pantheon.

An example of the latter was Vulcan/Gofannon. Vulcan (equivalent to the Greek Hephaestos) was the Roman god of the forge, beneficial fire, and volcanoes. In his role as divine smithy (blacksmith), he was an important weapons maker who provided other deities with spears, tridents, swords, and so forth. The Welsh deity Gofannon (called Goibniu in Ireland, Gobannus in Gaul, and possibly Gofannon or Gaban in England) was also a smithy god who made weapons. So when the Celts and Romans mingled in the first and second centuries A.D., they assumed that both peoples had been worshipping the same god under different names.

Boudica, queen of the Iceni, urges her troops to revolt against the Romans.

Two Magical Waterways

A number of striking similarities exist between certain ancient Celtic myths and gods and some Greco-Roman legends and deities. For example, the Greek nymph (minor goddess) Thetis's biggest claim to fame was that she was the mother of Achilles, the chief warrior-hero of the Trojan War. When Achilles was a baby, she held him by one heel and dipped him into the waters of the River Styx, the magical waterway bordering the dark Underworld. Thereafter, his body (except for the heel) was invulnerable to injury, allowing him to enter battle without fear of dying. A simi-

lar magical waterway appears in an old Celtic tale of a war between some benevolent gods, the Tuatha, and some monstrous deities, the nefarious Fomorians. The spring of Dian Cecht, the Tuatha god of medicine, contained water that could heal any and all wounds, thereby restoring someone who had been injured, or even killed, to health and life. So whenever one of the Tuatha was wounded or killed in battle, Dian Cecht dipped his or her body in the mystical spring. The patient soon emerged completely whole and reentered the fray against the enemy.

The Greek nymph Thetis dips her son Achilles in the River Styx, making him invulnerable to injury.

The Anglo-Saxon and Norse Deities

The similarities between separate groups of gods were even more marked in the cases of the pantheons of the Anglo-Saxons, Norse, and other Germanic peoples who entered Britain and displaced the Celts and Romans. Not only were their deities comparable or closely related, they also shared numerous myths that reflected real-life historical events or social customs.

One example was the well-known tale of the groups of ancient gods the Norse called the Aesir and Vanir and the pre-Christian Anglo-Saxons in Britain called the Ese and Wen (pronounced VEN). In the myth the two groups went to war. But over time neither side was victorious, so eventually they merged into a single pantheon led by Odin/Woden. Most modern experts believe that this myth had important historical and cultural overtones. They suggest that the Vanir/Wen were originally the peaceful fertility gods of the early non-Celtic northern European tribes. In contrast, the Aesir/Ese, many of whom were vigorous warrior gods, were the deities worshipped by the Indo-European tribes that migrated into northern Europe from western Asia. Just as it happened in the myth, in the faiths of the early northern European tribes these groups of gods combined over time, producing the classic Norse pantheon of gods.

Another myth associated with the Vanir/Wen and Aesir/Ese told how they merged. The deities in each group spit into a single jar and allowed the contents to thoroughly mingle. Soon, the divine spittle grew into a new god named Kvasir, who bore traits of all the others and thereby became the wisest of all of them. Supremely honorable and honest, he officially witnessed, or oversaw, the truce and the oaths sworn by the members of each group to remain allies forever. For the Norse and Anglo-Saxons who dwelled in medieval Britain, the myth of Kvasir was socially central and retold often. This is because

Kvasir's Blood

In a myth about the wise and poetic god Kvasir, he was murdered by two nefarious dwarfs, who then drained his blood. They mixed the blood with honey to produce a sweet-tasting wine called mead. Thereafter, it was said that drinking mead could make a person a poet or scholar.

it illustrated the importance of swearing oaths and in particular of *witnessing* the rituals of forging agreements and other kinds of oath taking.

Another example of a myth about an Anglo-Saxon god that had significance to people in their daily lives was the famous tale of Thunor's lost hammer. The mighty god of thunder awoke one morning to discover that his chief weapon and symbol, his matchless, invincible hammer, was missing. Thunor was sure that one of the giants, who were sworn enemies of the gods, was the culprit. He went to Loki, the divine trickster, and asked for help. The plan they agreed on was for Loki to use his unusually wide knowledge of the giants to locate the hammer, after which Thunor would provide the muscle and fighting skills needed to retrieve it. After a while Loki did manage to find the lost object. It turned out that the king of the giants, Thrym, had swiped it while Thunor was sleeping.

At the suggestion of another god, Thunor dressed as a woman to gain access to Thrym's abode, situated inside of a mountain in Giantland. The disguised Thunor pretended to agree to marry the giant, and a few days later large numbers of giants attended the wedding ceremony. Thinking he was giving a gift to his soon-to-be bride, the dim-witted Thrym laid the stolen hammer right in Thunor's lap. At the appropriate moment, the god of thunder threw off his costume and swung the great weapon in a swift stroke that crushed the giant's skull. Thunor then proceeded to slay the rest of the giants in the hall, after which he returned in triumph to Asgard, the home of the gods.

Archaeological and literary evidence shows that Thunor's hammer carried a great deal of symbolic power in ancient and medieval Germanic society. Large numbers of people, including some in medieval England, wore amulets shaped like that hammer to ward off evil. The image of Thunor's hammer was also invoked in important ceremonies to make them holy. For example, the Norse who settled in England, and possibly some early Anglo-Saxons in that area, employed a ritual hammer in the same manner that it was used in the myth. Just as Thrym gave the disguised Thunor the hammer in Giantland, during a Norse or Anglo-Saxon wedding

The Saxon god of thunder, Thunor, is closely associated with the Norse thunder god, Thor. Both wielded a great hammer.

ceremony, the groom placed a hammer symbolic of Thunor's in the bride's lap. Also, similar ritual hammers were used to bless babies' births, sacred feasts, and the funeral pyres of the dead.

Other holy objects associated with Thunor/Thor and his myths reveal certain aspects of early Anglo-Saxon worship and everyday life. First, the tales of the deity's fights with a horrible giant named Hrungnir and other enemies, along with artistic depictions of these events in temples dedicated to the god, may have been related to initiation ceremonies. Some scholars think that a young person entering the temple's congregation went through a mock battle with a worshipper dressed as a giant. When the initiate pretended to slay his opponent (who likely cried out and feigned dying at the appropriate moment), he was welcomed into the group.

Also, Thunor's holy rings were used by worshippers during rituals in which they swore oaths to both members of

This illustration depicts the Vikings submitting to Alfred the Great by taking a sacred oath, which they swore on Thunor's rings that they would keep.

the community and outsiders. The *Anglo-Saxon Chronicle*, which English scribes began compiling in about A.D. 890 at the request of their ruler Alfred the Great, describes an example of such oath taking. In 876, it says, some Vikings who had attacked England made a truce with Alfred, and all those involved swore on Thunor's rings to stay true to their word. To break a promise made upon these rings was viewed as an extremely vile crime and punishable by death.

In these and other ways, the myths that described the gods of the early peoples who settled in Britain were often reflected in the social customs, beliefs, and other realities of everyday life. People first heard the stories of the gods and their adventures when they were small children. When they grew up, they passed these tales along to their own children. This caused various aspects of the myths to become ingrained in society in the form of social customs such as grooms placing hammers in their wives' laps. From this fact, one can see how difficult it was when the Anglo-Saxons eventually adopted Christian beliefs. Although they rejected the old gods, the enduring social customs connected to the characters were constant reminders of the people's proud and memorable past.

CHAPTER 3

Legends of Beloved Human Heroes

Although the peoples of ancient and medieval Britain venerated and perpetuated the myths surrounding their gods, they were even more captivated by their legends of a group of beloved human heroes. Each succeeding wave of invaders and settlers had its favorite heroic characters. The colorful deeds the heroes performed often reflected various religious beliefs or cultural aspects of those who told and retold their tales. As these peoples steadily came together, creating the beginnings of what would become modern Britain, local folk heroes from diverse cultures became part of a larger British mythology. The late British scholar M.I. Ebbutt wrote:

> In the hero-legends of [Britain] we may find traces of the thoughts and religions of our ancestors many centuries ago, traces which lie close to one another in these romances, telling of the nations [that is, peoples] who came to these Islands of the West, settled, and were conquered and driven away to make room for other races whose supremacy has been as brief, till all these superimposed races have blended into one, to form the British nation.[21]

The Celebrated Beowulf

In this way heroes that were initially known only to one or two cultural groups eventually became famous all over Britain and well beyond. Among the most celebrated of all these characters is Beowulf. Originally an Anglo-Saxon hero, his myth was for an unknown number of centuries passed along orally. At some point in the mid-medieval period—perhaps around A.D. 1000—it was written down in the form of a long poem by an anonymous storyteller.

Although written in Britain in Old English, the setting of *Beowulf* is ancient Denmark. The first of its three main characters is Hrothgar, a Danish king who erected a magnificent "hall," a large building where a ruler and his nobles met, held court, and feasted. The second leading character is Beowulf, a brave warrior from the land of the Geats, now southern Sweden. He "plays Superman" in the story, educator and scholar Chris Vinsonhaler remarks. "His fantastic strength would delight a popular audience, especially in a male-dominant culture." The third character is Grendel, a hideous combination of man and beast whose hide cannot be pierced by ordinary weapons. In Vinsonhaler's words:

> Grendel is a superb monster with the grotesque appeal of a Frankenstein. Because he is more man than monster, the horror of his savagery creates a high level of identification. The poem's ability to manipulate folkloric elements is especially evident when we imagine the context of its telling. The audience might well have listened to the story of a monster attacking a [hall] at night, while sitting in a [hall] at night. The poet shows a masterful ability to enthrall the audience by saying, "BOO!"[22]

Not long after Hrothgar established his court in his great hall, the tale begins, Grendel appeared seemingly out of nowhere and devoured several of the Danish nobles. This proved to be only the beginning of a campaign of terror. The man-beast, who dwelled in a cave situated underneath a lake, launched more such grisly attacks, throwing the kingdom into a state of abject fear. Soon, however, news of these events reached Beowulf and his fourteen trusty knights. They hurried to Denmark and offered their services to King Hrothgar, promising to rid the land of the menacing creature.

Having hatched a plan, Beowulf and his men went to Hrothgar's empty hall and lay in wait for Grendel. Sure enough, the monster arrived and immediately assaulted one of the Geats. Springing forward, Beowulf seized Grendel, and the two wrestled furiously while the other warriors tried but failed to cut into the creature's body with their swords. Finally, Beowulf managed to tear off one of his opponent's arms. Screeching loudly, Grendel retreated to his lair, where he soon died.

Beowulf rips off the arm of the monster Grendel in Hrothgar's great hall.

Thinking that the kingdom was now safe, everyone rejoiced and celebrated. But they were mistaken. It turned out that Grendel's equally repulsive mother also lived in the cave, and she became determined to avenge her son's demise. She kidnapped and ate one of Hrothgar's leading officials, after which Beowulf and his followers tracked her to the lake. Beowulf fearlessly dove into the water, reached the subterranean chamber, and engaged in a fight to the death with Grendel's mother, eventually beheading her.

The Hero's Rules

On its surface Beowulf's myth was, and remains, pure entertainment. In medieval times roving minstrels told and retold it, often adding new plot details and atmospheric touches until it was finally written down and attained its present form. Over time it came to be seen as one of Western civilization's classic adventure tales.

Beneath that colorful surface, however, the tale both reflected and reinforced some of the more basic cultural values of the Anglo-Saxons and other Germanic peoples who lived in Scandinavia and Britain. Of these, the most important was the Germanic heroic code, or *comitatus*. It was essentially a set of rules that accumulated over time, righteous customs that warriors were expected to follow, even if some of their number at times failed to do so. The ideal warrior was a strong, courageous defender of his society and its rulers, willing to give his life for both. He was not only loyal, but also honest and just, and he treated others with decency and compassion.

These warrior ideals quite naturally made their way into various myths, including that of Beowulf. He and his men personified what average folk viewed as the most admirable people, individuals to be looked up to and glorified. Following is one of several passages in the tale that extol their virtues. After following the wounded Grendel's tracks to the lake and realizing he must be dead, "the brave warriors

Beowulf Survives

Experts think that the original manuscript telling Beowulf's tale was written sometime between the early 700s and the year 1000. It survived a 1737 fire that destroyed much of the library in which it rested, although the edges of most of the pages were scorched. The manuscript was restored as best as was then possible about a century later.

Defending One's Leader to the Death

One of the warrior ideals contained in the Germanic heroic code, the comitatus, *was that a worthy warrior should defend his leader to his utmost, even laying down his life in the process. In fact, if a warrior survived a battle in which his leader was slain, it was assumed that the warrior had not tried hard enough to avenge the leader. In his study of cultural and literary heroes, University of Rochester scholar Dean A. Miller states:*

The *comitatus* was held together . . . by mutual oaths sworn to and by the war band leader, and one of these obligated the warriors not to survive their fallen chieftain. . . . Here, what we can probably call a quasi-religious sanction calls for the deaths—in truth, the sacrifice—of the whole war band when its leader fell. The chieftain's death demands a full payment or toll of lives, including—but not only—the lives of his foes.

Dean A. Miller. *The Epic Hero.* Baltimore: Johns Hopkins University Press, 2000, pp. 339–340.

rode back [to Hrothgar's hall] on their gleaming horses from this joyful journey. Then Beowulf's exploit was acclaimed. Many a man asserted time and again that there was no better shield-bearer in the whole world, to north or south between the two seas, under the sky's expanse, no man more worthy of his own kingdom."[23]

Such passages thrilled the Anglo-Saxons and later all Britons—nobles and commoners alike—as they read or listened to someone recite Beowulf's myth. More specific references to the courage of his knights appear in the action and battle scenes. In their first fight with Grendel, for example, the warriors are unable to penetrate the beast's skin with their swords, yet they relentlessly continue to try, risking their own lives to save their leader. "Time and again,

Beowulf's band brandished their ancestral swords, [longing] to save the life, if they so could, of their lord, the mighty leader. . . . They struck at the monster from every side, eager for his end."[24]

Similarly, after Beowulf dives into the lake, for close to an hour no one knows whether he is alive or dead. His men have no way of knowing that he made it past the water

This eighth-century illuminated manuscript is a page from the epic poem Beowulf. *It is the earliest surviving account of the myth of the hero Beowulf.*

to the cave, and they are aware that humans cannot hold their breath underwater that long. Yet rather than abandon Beowulf, his men remain at the water's edge the whole time, selflessly exposing themselves to the possible reappearance of the monster. True, no gruesome creatures like Grendel and his monstrous mother actually existed in Scandinavia or Britain in those days. But this myth and others like it reassured average people that among their own ranks were fearless fighters who could and would defend them against whatever real dangers they might confront.

Culhwch's Quest for Love

Like the Anglo-Saxons and other Germanic peoples who settled in what is now England, the Celts who dwelled in Britain had their own local mythical heroes. In Wales, for instance, one of the most admired of these champions was an intrepid knight named Culhwch. He was best known for his quest to find and marry Olwen, a beautiful young woman. Culhwch was the son of a legendary Welsh monarch, King Cilydd, whose first wife, Culhwch's mother, died young. The king eventually took a second wife, who became both queen and Culhwch's stepmother.

One day the new queen tried to persuade Culhwch to marry her daughter, his stepsister, but he refused. Offended, the queen retaliated by putting a spell on the young man, one that convinced him that he was fated to marry a particular young woman. "I declare to you," the queen said, "that it is your destiny not to be wedded to a wife until you obtain Olwen, the daughter of Ysbaddaden, the chief of the giants." Immediately, Culhwch began to pine away for Olwen, a woman he had never seen but who was known to be attractive despite her father's ugliness. King Cilydd saw the change in his son's mood and asked, "What has come over you, my son, and what is wrong with you?"[25] The blushing young man replied, "My stepmother has declared to me that I shall never have a wife until I obtain Olwen."[26]

The king informed his son that it would not be easy to convince Olwen to marry him. This was because her monstrous, one-eyed father was extremely ornery, did not like strangers, and kept his daughter well-guarded behind his

Culhwch Catches Sight of Olwen

In the myth of Culhwch and Olwen, soon after the young man reached the castle of the maid's monstrous father, Olwen snuck out to meet her suitor. The beautiful vision Culhwch beheld when he first caught sight of her was recorded in the old Welsh romance, the *Mabinogion*: "She arrived wearing a robe of flame-red silk about her, and around her neck a choker of red gold imbedded with precious pearls and rubies. . . . Whiter was her flesh than the foam of the wave. . . . Whiter were her breasts than the breast of the white swan. Redder were her cheeks than the reddest foxgloves. Who so beheld her would be filled with love for her."

Quoted in Richard Barber, ed. *The Arthurian Legends: An Illustrated Anthology*. Rochester, NY: Boydell, 1996, p. 36.

This scene from the Mabinogion *shows Olwen, wearing a robe of flame-coloured silk.*

castle walls. Culhwch knew that his father was right. But the young man was still filled with desire to marry Olwen. So he went to King Cilydd's cousin, the English ruler King Arthur, and asked for his help.

Arthur saw and sympathized with Culhwch's plight and sent some of his knights to aid him in his quest. They arranged for the young man to have a meeting with Olwen, who snuck out of her father's castle for that purpose. She felt love for Culhwch at first sight and was amenable to marrying him. But she warned him that her father would never consent, so she feared there was no way the wedding would happen.

Culhwch remained determined to have Olwen as his wife, however. So he went to Ysbaddaden and told him just that. The giant frowned and proceeded to impose a long list of incredibly difficult tasks for the young man to perform. Only when Culhwch had completed all those tasks, the giant thundered, would he have a chance of marrying Olwen. Undeterred by these demands and very sure of himself, Culhwch looked Ysbaddaden in his single eye and said softly and simply, "I shall gain your daughter, and you shall lose your life."[27]

Culhwch's threat came to pass. He slew the giant and married his daughter. Though exaggerated, some of the marriage customs described in this myth mirrored real ones practiced in ancient Celtic societies. Culhwch had to approach Olwen's father to ask permission to wed her because her father had the final say in who she could marry. Often, fathers in upper-class Celtic families arranged the marriages of their daughters by negotiating with the fathers of young men.

Also, in some Celtic groups, a groom-to-be was expected to perform some sort of difficult or heroic act before he could obtain permission to marry a young woman. In the myth Ysbaddaden demanded that Culhwch move a nearby hill, plow a huge field, and plant crops in the field, all in the space of a single day. The giant also said that the young man must find a batch of honey nine times sweeter than the ordinary kind and yank out the tusk of a gigantic, raging boar. Similarly, in some Celtic tribes a prospective husband was asked to first perform a feat requiring strength, skill, or bravery—or all of these. Hunting and killing a dangerous wild animal, a parallel to the giant boar in the myth, was typical.

Of Kings, Love, and War

Kings, lords of castles, and young princesses are also prominent in another early British myth—that of King Leir. The story was later adapted, with a few small changes, by English playwright William Shakespeare in his play *King Lear*, written between 1603 and 1606. In the legend Leir was a venerable old monarch who had no son to inherit the throne upon his death. He did have three daughters, however. Their names were Goneril, Regan, and Cordelia. Goneril was mar-

ried to the Duke of Albany, and Regan's husband was the Duke of Cornwall. Cordelia was yet unmarried.

The king was unsure which daughter he should leave his kingdom to in his will. So he finally decided that the three women would divide the kingdom in equal parts after his passing. To celebrate his decision, Leir held a special ceremony in which each daughter publicly reaffirmed her love and respect for her father. Goneril and Regan heaped praises on him. The first said she loved her father more than her own soul, and the other claimed she loved him more than anyone else in the whole world. But they were lying. They did not really love him and said these things only to stay in his good graces and make sure they would later inherit their shares of the realm.

King Lear weeps over the body of his daughter Cordelia in this painting of a scene from Shakespeare's play King Lear, *which was based on the ancient British myths of King Leir.*

As for Cordelia, she actually did love her father. But she felt it was dishonest for her to say she loved him any more than was natural for a daughter to care for a parent. So she refused to lie, and instead stated, "As far as I am concerned, I have always loved you as a father, and will always do so. You want me to say more, but listen to the true measure of my love. This is my answer. Just as you are worth whatever you possess, so I love you for what you are."[28]

King Leir totally misunderstood what his third daughter was trying to tell him. He interpreted her truthful words to mean that she did not love him as much as her sisters did. So he disinherited Cordelia and announced that Goneril and Regan would each inherit half the kingdom. Moreover, even before his death, they could temporarily divide and rule half the realm while Leir himself ruled the other half.

This arrangement proved to be Leir's downfall. Not long afterward, the Dukes of Albany and Cornwall, urged on by Goneril and Regan, rebelled and seized the entire kingdom. At first, out of sympathy, Albany maintained the aged king, assigning sixty knights to care for his needs. But Goneril, who now thought nothing of admitting she had no feelings for her father, reduced this number to thirty. Indignant, Leir ran to Cornwall and Regan's castle in hopes of receiving better treatment. But there, Regan further reduced the number of his bodyguards to five.

Finally, Leir saw how wrong he had been about his daughters' true feelings for him. Realizing now that Cordelia was the only one who actually loved him, he sought her out. By this time she was married to Aganippus, king of the Franks (in Gaul, what is now France), and she welcomed her father with open arms. Now, Leir, Aganippus, and Cordelia raised an army, crossed the English Channel, and defeated Albany's and Cornwall's forces. Leir was reinstated on the English throne and ruled several more years, after which Cordelia succeeded him as England's ruler.

Modern scholars think that this moving ancient tale may well reflect some of the real relationships among early British rulers and their families. The events portrayed in the myth depict how unreliable and disloyal a royal daughter or son could be to her or his father, often because of greed for land, lust for power, or both. The myth was also a powerful reminder to ordinary early Britons that kings and queens were not god-like or perfect. Like everyone else, they sometimes made serious mistakes. Also, no matter how powerful a king was, he had to deal with the feelings and actions of his own children, which could lead to his downfall. Moreover, like all human beings, kings could feel fear and despair and lead troubled lives. Thus, to some degree the myth humanized royalty in the eyes of average people.

Perhaps more importantly, the myth of King Leir also showed the early inhabitants of Britain the dangers of having an unstable ruler. When Leir fled to Gaul and came back to England with an army to overthrow his disloyal daughters and their husbands, thousands of ordinary people either died or lost loved ones, their homes, and/or their feelings of security. This was likely as common an occurrence in ancient Britain as it was in various periods of medieval Britain. Indeed, the fact that war is a major theme in many old British myths no doubt indicates that wars were fairly frequent in early British history.

To Bring Justice to All

The myths of Beowulf, Culhwch, and King Leir are very old, as experts date them to the first few medieval centuries or earlier. A good deal younger, as British myths go, although no less popular and beloved, were the tales of Robin Hood, said to be an outlaw who robbed from the rich to give to the poor. In the most highly developed versions of the myth, Robin dwelled with his followers, the "Merry Men," among them Little John, in Sherwood Forest in the county of Nottinghamshire in central England. He had originally been a nobleman. But he had lost his lands due to corrupt practices by high government officials, notably the scheming King John and his sinister henchman the sheriff of Nottingham. "Feared by the bad" and

Sherwood Infested

A formerly unknown medieval mention of Robin Hood was discovered in 2009 in an inscription dating from about 1460. Apparently penned by monks who disapproved of Robin, it reads: "Around this time, according to popular opinion, a certain outlaw named Robin Hood, with his accomplices, infested Sherwood and other law-abiding areas of England with continuous robberies."

Little John knocks Robin Hood into the river in the popular myth of Robin Hood. John became one of Robin's "Merry Men" who dwelled in Sherwood Forest.

"loved by the good,"[29] Robin fought for justice and the rights of the poor and underprivileged.

This familiar scenario, or variations of it, have been portrayed in countless poems, novels, and movies over the years. Although entertaining, many of its elements were later additions, some of them inserted in the past three centuries. For example, Robin did not always dwell in Sherwood Forest, nor did he always live in the time of King John (the late 1100s), nor was he always viewed as good or righteous. In fact, the earliest versions of the myth simply picture him as an outlaw who hid out in a forest and, with a small band of followers, lived off the land and whatever they could steal.

Robin was first mentioned, only in passing, in a literary work written in 1377 and a chronicle dated to around 1420. The first substantial written telling of his exploits was a ballad titled "Robin Hood and the Monk," penned around 1450. Also dating roughly to this period are records of real outlaws who took the names Robin Hood and Little John in an attempt to enhance their reputations. Modern scholars think the original legend of Robin Hood appeared a bit earlier than these written versions, perhaps the mid- to late 1200s.

The first substantial literary mention of Robin Hood is a ballad dating from 1420 called "Robin Hood and the Monk." This lithograph depicts one of their meetings.

More or less, this is all that modern scholars know for certain about Robin Hood. No reliable records have survived indicating that the original legend is based on a real person. Moreover, some experts think his mythical persona was patched together from tales of several individuals living in different places and eras.

Some other researchers go further and suggest that Robin Hood's legend was itself based on much older and more mystical myths. According to one theory, his character was a human version of the "King of the Wood," the companion of an ancient hunting goddess. That woodland king was said to die in early winter but then to return, as leaves and other

Robin Hood may be linked to the ancient myth of the King of the Wood. It explains why Robin lived in the forest and wore green clothing in later versions of the myth.

greenery do, each spring. This supposedly explains why in his later, more developed myth—that of Robin Hood—he felt so at home in the forest and always wore green clothing.

Wherever the tales of the honorable outlaw Robin Hood came from, those English who told and retold them in the 1400s, 1500s, and 1600s felt that these tales occupied an important place in both their culture and their hearts. Put simply, Robin was an anti-authority figure. He stood for and held out the promise that lower-class folk who felt repressed and/or exploited by overbearing nobles or unfair tax laws had a champion. Thus, cherishing and perpetuating Robin Hood's myth was a way for society's underprivileged to vent their frustrations and anxieties without resorting to armed rebellion. In this view, Robin and his efforts to bring justice to all were a sort of "anti-authoritarian safety valve,"[30] as noted Robin Hood scholar Stephen Knight phrases it. Another expert, military historian Mike Ibeji, elaborates:

> If the existing order [in medieval England] was founded on the arbitrary will of evil men who could twist the law to their own ends, then it was the role of the outlaw to seek redress and justice by other means. In a violent age, these means were invariably violent. Robin Hood and his contemporaries were cunning, merciless and often brutal . . . but by the codes of their time, they were also honorable.[31]

Indeed, to the credit of all the British heroes of old, one trait they held in common was a deeply felt and frequently demonstrated sense of honor.

CHAPTER 4

Britain's Most Popular Character

L ike the myths of the ancient Greeks and Romans, those of the ancient and medieval British contained numerous colorful, courageous, larger-than-life warriors. These heroes fought to rid the land of monsters, tyrants, and invaders or sought to win the love of a beautiful woman. Among the many British champions who fit that description, Beowulf, Culhwch, and Robin Hood were some of the greatest and best known.

However, none of Britain's mythical heroes was as famous, accomplished, and fondly remembered as King Arthur. Indeed, citing his exceptional valor, virtue, and honor, noted Arthurian scholar Graham Phillips calls him "arguably the most popular character in British history."[32] Other experts have gone even further. Along with Julius Caesar, Jesus Christ, Napoleon, and a handful of others, they say, Arthur is one of the most recognizable characters in the history of Western civilization.

Lord of Camelot

In his most fully developed myths, Arthur was lord of the fabled castle of Camelot—also the capital city of his realm, which stretched across large parts of England (although its exact location and size remain unknown). He commanded a group of morally upright knights who sat with him at the now renowned Round Table, at least when they were not out fighting villains and doing good deeds. Because the table was round, everyone who sat at it had an equal position, which symbolized that none was superior or inferior to the others. Also associated with Arthur were his wife and queen, Guinevere; his mentor, the mysterious magician Merlin; Sir Lancelot, a valiant French knight who became the king's closest friend but also had a love affair with the queen; and Arthur's son, Mordred, who eventually betrayed him, causing both their deaths and the demise of Camelot.

Collectively, the large number of myths describing these characters are frequently called the "Arthurian legends." They are also sometimes viewed as part of the Arthurian "mythos." A huge and diverse compilation, it includes not only the stories of the characters and their deeds, but also all of the historical chronicles, poems, books, plays, and

Sir Tristan swears allegiance to Arthur in this manuscript illumination. Arthur's knights sat with him at a round table, which showed that everyone held an equal position.

paintings portraying them over the centuries. It features, in addition, the many theories about Arthur's identity and the origins of his myths.

The Arthurian mythos is still expanding today as new literature, songs, movies, and other Arthur-related materials are continually introduced. But the original Arthurian legends from medieval Britain remain the bedrock, so to speak, of Arthurian studies and storytelling. Like all archaic myths, initially they were primarily passed along orally. But eventually they were set to paper in a series of early texts that either briefly mentioned people and events from the legends or described them in great detail. They include Nennius's *History of the Britons* (dating to the 800s); the *Welsh Annals*, a group of historical chronicles (900s); Geoffrey's *History of the Kings of Britain* (1100s); several French, German, and English romances, essentially long stories (1100s–1400s); and Englishman Thomas Malory's long, detailed romance, *Le Morte d'Arthur*, or *The Death of Arthur* (1485).

The True Son and Heir

One of the most memorable of the tales that emerged from those classic Arthurian primary sources was the story of Arthur's origins and how he became king. The tale begins in the distant past, when much of England was ruled by a powerful war leader named Uther Pendragon. Although he was capable and well meaning, his authority was regularly threatened. Ambitious, self-serving local warlords held sway in several parts of the land, while the crude Germanic Saxons launched periodic raids across the English Channel.

Realizing that his kingdom was unstable and he himself vulnerable to overthrow, Uther worried what might happen to any children he might have. He consulted his friend, the powerful magician Merlin, who revealed that

Guinevere's Exploits

Several different legends about Queen Guinevere exist, some of which provide slight variations of her exploits. Most often, following Arthur's discovery of her affair with Lancelot, she is condemned to be burned at the stake. But Lancelot rescues her at the last minute. Following Arthur's death, she enters a convent and remains there for the remainder of her life.

King Uther and his wife give the child Arthur into Merlin's protection. Merlin in turn gave the child to Sir Ector, who raised him as his own.

the king would soon have a son. Uther must permit Merlin to take the infant away, Merlin said, to be brought up by someone else. When the king started to object, the magician insisted that this odd arrangement would be best for the child's welfare. Since the safety of his offspring was then uppermost in Uther's mind, he reluctantly agreed.

Sure enough, not long afterward Uther's wife, Igraine, bore him a son, and Uther immediately ordered two of his knights to give the baby to the white-bearded, dark-robed Merlin. The latter secretly bore the boy to the home of Sir Ector, an upstanding knight. Ector and his wife named the child Arthur and in the years that followed came to love him no less than their biological son, Kay.

Merlin also took an active role in Arthur's upbringing, showing him how to shoot a bow, swim, and ride horses. Merlin also taught the young man a very unusual skill that only a sorcerer could know—talking to animals in their own tongues. The magician refrained from revealing to the boy that he was the king's true son and heir. Even after Uther Pendragon died and a number of powerful, ambitious nobles began to compete for the throne, Arthur continued to think he was Ector's son.

The Sword in the Stone

Several more years passed. Because the kingdom remained divided and disorganized, Merlin decided it was necessary for the real king to emerge and set things right. He asked the land's most widely respected religious leader, the Archbishop of Canterbury, to gather together all the vying English lords in London to celebrate Christmas. At that time a miracle would take place, Merlin predicted.

When Christmas arrived and the leading nobles and their chief knights entered London's main cathedral to pray, they spied something strange in the nearby churchyard. As Mal-

Early References to Arthur

The first actual historical references to Arthur appear in the anonymous *Welsh Annals* (*Annales Cambriae*) and the *History of the Britons* (*Historia Brittonum*). Both works are difficult to date, but the consensus of scholars is that they were written in the eighth or ninth century. The *Annals* consists of lists of dates, each followed by a short entry about an important event. Shown here are the two that mention Arthur.

[A.D. 518, the year of] the Battle of [Mount] Badon, in which Arthur bore the cross of our Lord Jesus Christ on his shoulders for three days and three nights, and the Britons were the victors.

[A.D. 539, the year of the] Battle of Camlann, in which Arthur and Medraut [Mordred] perished; and there was plague in Britain and Ireland.

Quoted in Richard Barber, ed. *The Arthurian Legends: An Illustrated Anthology.* Rochester, NY: Boydell, 1996, p. 7.

ory described it, it was a large marble stone in the middle of which loomed "an anvil of steel, a foot in height, and therein stuck a fair sword." On the sword, gold lettering marked out the following message: "Whoever pulls this sword out of this stone and anvil is rightly King of all England."[33]

Eager to prove himself, each of the rival lords attempted to remove the sword from the stone. But no one could. The archbishop then stated the obvious—that none of the competitors could be the true king. The best course, the churchman said, would be to stage a tournament in which the greatest nobles and knights in the kingdom would joust with one another. The winner of these mock fights would clearly be the realm's leading warrior and thereby worthy of becoming king.

So it came to pass that dozens of strong and bold men of arms gathered at London's jousting field to compete for the kingship. Ector was among them, as was his son Kay, now in his late teens. Arthur, who was in his early teens, acted as his brother's squire, or helper. While preparing for the jousting, Kay realized to his dismay that he had left his sword at home, and Arthur offered to hurry back and get it. When he arrived at Ector's castle, however, the sword was not there.

Arthur Removes the Sword

Upset that without a sword Kay would not be allowed to fight in the tournament, Arthur frantically thought about where he might find a suitable sword. Then he remembered that while attending church he had seen a magnificent sword imbedded in a stone in the cathedral's churchyard. Leaping back on his horse, he rode to the cathedral and entered the churchyard, which at that moment was deserted. The boy walked to the stone, clutched the sword's hilt, pulled, and was relieved to see that the weapon easily slipped out.

A few minutes later, Arthur entered Kay's tent at the jousting field and gave him the sword. Both Kay and his father noted the weapon's unusual beauty and asked where it had come from, to which Arthur answered that he had pulled it from the stone in the churchyard. Rushing to the cathedral, Ector saw for himself that the sword that had earlier projected from the stone was indeed missing. He realized

After the lords and knights had all failed to draw the sword from the stone, Arthur stepped up and effortlessly drew the sword out. He was thus declared king on the spot.

what this meant, namely that his younger son was England's true king.

Ector immediately informed the archbishop of the miracle in the churchyard, and the churchman urged all of the nobles and knights to assemble as swiftly as possible at the cathedral. While everyone watched, Ector replaced the sword. Then each lord and knight took his turn, as before, at trying to draw the weapon from the marble slab. Also as before, they all failed.

Finally, at the archbishop's nod, Arthur stepped up to the stone and, seemingly effortlessly, pulled the sword out. A hush came over the crowd as all present stared in astonishment. Then one of the nobles shouted, "We will have Arthur as our king!" The other warriors excitedly repeated those words and almost in unison added, "We all see that it is God's will that he shall be our king, and whoever opposes it we will slay!"[34] Soon afterward, in a splendid ceremony, the archbishop placed the royal crown on Arthur's head, and his reign, which would be remembered for all time, began.

Excalibur and the Holy Grail

This charming myth explaining how Arthur became king is only one of the numerous colorful tales about his legendary rule. Another tells how he came by his famous sword known as Excalibur. Arthur and Merlin were riding beside a lake when they saw an arm with a sword in its hand rise up from the water. The arm belonged to the Lady of the Lake, a woman whom Merlin knew well and who helped Arthur and some of his knights from time to time. After the sword rose from the water, a strange woman appeared on the shore, walked atop the water's surface, retrieved the weapon, and brought it to Arthur. This tale received appropriate closure later, when, following his final battle, the wounded Arthur handed Excalibur to one of his most trusted knights, Sir Bedivere. The king ordered the knight to throw it into the lake. When Bedivere slung the sword out over the water, the Lady of the Lake's arm suddenly reappeared and caught the weapon.

Another famous Arthurian story recalls how several of Arthur's knights went in search of the Holy Grail, the cup supposedly used by Jesus at the Last Supper. After many adventures and hardships, however, one by one the mighty warriors failed in their quests. Only Sir Lancelot's son, Sir Galahad, who was pure of heart, succeeded in locating the cup, after which he rose up into heaven.

Other Arthurian myths describe Arthur's battles, including his decisive

The Grail's First Appearance

The sacred chalice called the Holy Grail first appears in Camelot in the midst of a bright flash of light in the large hall where Arthur and the members of his royal court are meeting. As they watch in amazement, the object floats around the hall, causing food to appear in everyone's dishes, and then disappears as quickly as it came.

The Several Ladies of the Lake

The mystical and often fleeting Lady of the Lake appeared as several distinct characters in different versions of the King Arthur myths. In one version, in which she is called Viviane, she entices the magician Merlin to teach her what he knows about magical spells and lore and then uses this knowledge to trap him inside a tree trunk. In other Arthurian stories the Lady of the Lake is Ninianne, who gives Arthur his sword Excalibur. By contrast, in Thomas Malory's version of the Arthurian tales, the woman who provides Arthur with the sword is called Nimue. She temporarily takes Merlin's place as Arthur's adviser, and later, after the bloody battle in which Arthur fights his son, Mordred, she takes back Excalibur. In addition, another Arthurian story features the Lady of the Lake as one of the four queens who transports the wounded Arthur to the legendary Isle of Avalon.

In the legend of King Arthur, the sword Excalibur is given to Arthur by Ninianne, the Lady of the Lake.

victory over the Saxons at Mount Badon. His last battle was at Camlann. There, he and his son, Mordred, who had attempted to usurp the throne, opposed each other, and the loss of most of the king's knights in the conflict brought about the demise of the fellowship of the Round Table. Mordred was slain and Arthur was mortally wounded. In a follow-up tale, a group of women carried the stricken ruler to the mysterious Isle of Avalon. In one version of the myth, he died there. In another he was healed and thereafter awaited a call to return in some future age and rule Britain once again.

All of Arthur's knights failed in their search for the Holy Grail, except for Sir Galahad. Pure of heart, Galahad ascended to heaven after he found the cup.

A Proud Cultural Heritage

For the inhabitants of medieval and early modern Britain, these Arthurian tales were both compelling and entertaining. On the one hand it was a welcome escape from long hours of work for ordinary folk to occasionally hear minstrels recite these romantic stories. Hearing about how powerful, attractive men and women once participated in larger-than-life events might make a person briefly forget about his or her every-day problems.

On the other hand, the Arthurian myths repeatedly dealt with themes such as chivalry, loyalty, justice, courage, fairness, and respect and love for God. These were qualities that average people wanted to see in their own rulers, society, and personal lives. They knew full well that not everyone was brave, just, or pious or even capable of being so. Yet they were convinced that at least some individuals in each new generation did possess these qualities. Moreover, they

A fifteenth-century illuminated manuscript shows Arthur and his knights arriving at the castle in Camelot.

were proud to have a cultural heritage that recalled a time when large numbers of their ancestors supposedly had these special traits.

Beyond these general ways of viewing the Arthurian myths, it is difficult to gauge how they more specifically both affected and reflected the culture and lives of the medieval British. In part this is because the Arthurian legends appeared and accumulated over many centuries. During that long interval medieval society evolved and changed considerably, and it is hard to know in which period the events and customs described in the myths belong.

For example, by the time the Arthurian romances were written, the stone castles, heavily armored knights, and codes of chivalry described in those works were commonplace in Europe. The problem is that the individuals who wrote the romances assumed that such cultural aspects had existed for many hundreds of years. But this was not the case. Stone castles and heavily armored knights did not begin to appear in Britain, or in Europe in general, until after the Norman Conquest in 1066. Geoffrey Ashe writes, "With the Arthur story, characters in an [age] which the authors knew quite well to be ancient were still dressed up as knights and ladies appropriate to the twelfth or thirteenth century. Neither Arthur nor any of his circle would have been like that."[35]

Was Arthur a Real Person?

Thus, in order to ascertain how the Arthurian myths reflected various aspects of society, one must first try to determine when Arthur lived. One promising approach is to find a specific period of medieval Britain in which customs, religious beliefs, and other cultural features were the same or similar to those in the myths. The existence of such similarities would strongly argue that Arthur's myths, and by extension all myths, contain reflections of the peoples, customs, and beliefs of the societies that generated them.

Morgan le Fay

One of the major characters in the Arthurian legends of the late Middle Ages was Arthur's half sister Morgan le Fay. Several of these tales depict her opposing the Round Table and causing trouble among Arthur's knights. In the end, however, she makes amends with her brother and becomes one of the women who bear him to Avalon following his mortal wounding at Camlann.

Was Winchester Camelot?

Arthur's Round Table was one of his most renowned trademarks. Several British towns today claim to own the table or pieces of it. Among these is the Winchester Round Table, measuring 18 feet (5.5m) in diameter and made of oak, located in the great hall of Winchester Castle (southeast of London). The locals are quick to point out that Thomas Malory thought Winchester was the site of Camelot. Also, they say, Malory's publisher, William Caxton, believed the table at Winchester was Arthur's. The English ruler during Caxton's time, King Henry VII (reigned 1485–1509), accepted this argument and decided to use the Winchester Round Table to boost his and his family's prestige and popularity. In 1486 he transported his pregnant wife to Winchester, where she soon bore him a son. They named the baby Arthur II for obvious propaganda purposes. However, Henry's romantic dreams of uniting England in his version of a new age of Camelot were foiled when Arthur suddenly died, of uncertain causes, in 1502 at the age of fifteen.

English author of Arthurian tales Thomas Malory believed that Winchester Castle (shown in 2007) was Arthur's castle at Camelot.

Of course, this assumes that Arthur was indeed a real person, which remains uncertain. Some historians think he was most likely a purely mythical figure. However, a growing number of scholars feel his legends may have been based on real people and events and that those stories became highly exaggerated over time. As English researcher Philip Wilkinson puts it, "The mythical King Arthur, famed as Briton's brave and virtuous leader, was probably based on a real person."[36] Ashe agrees and adds that Arthur "belongs in the late fifth century or the early sixth, a mysterious phase after Britain broke away from the Roman Empire."[37]

From Scythia to Camelot

Following this logical reasoning, scholars have proposed a number of candidates for the historical Arthur, all from Britain's immediate post-Roman period. One of the strongest contenders was proposed in 1994 by scholars C. Scott Littleton and Linda A. Malcor. They point out that in the late second century, the Roman emperor Marcus Aurelius (reigned A.D. 161–180) battled and defeated a group of tribes living on the steppes of Scythia, which included what is now southern Ukraine. Among them were the Sarmatians, who were excellent cavalrymen (mounted warriors). Not long afterward, Aurelius hired some eight thousand Sarmatian fighters to bolster the Roman army ranks, and about fifty-five hundred of them were assigned to Roman Britain.

At this point, the striking parallels between myth and history begin. First, the British Sarmatians were commanded by Lucius Artorius Castus, and *Artorius* is the Latin version of "Arthur." Also, the Sarmatian horsemen fought with lances, just as Arthur's mythical knights did. As standards, the Sarmatians carried banners displaying dragons. Both Arthur and his father, Uther Pendragon, used such banners, and the name *Pendragon* means "dragon's head."

Moreover, one of the central religious images employed in Sarmatian worship was a large sword with its blade imbedded in a stone, and a popular Scythian myth tells about a warrior who had to throw his sword into the sea just before he died, a scenario almost identical to the Arthurian tale in which, prior to his own passing, Arthur ordered Sir Bedivere to sling Excalibur into a lake. In addition, as noted Arthurian expert John Matthews points out, "Evidence tells of a Sarmatian contingent garrisoned at the fort of Camboglanna [in northern England], which . . . may have been the site of Arthur's last battle at Camlann, or even the original Camelot."[38]

Based on these and numerous other close analogies, some experts say it is possible that when the Romans abandoned Britain in the early 400s, a Sarmatian-Roman community—descended from the original Sarmatians posted in Britain—still existed there. Its members banded together, maybe along with other locals, to defend their homes and way of life against the invading Saxons, as well as criminal elements that were flourishing in the wake of the Roman army's withdrawal. The leader of the community may have been a descendant and namesake of the second-century Artorius. Or perhaps that leader, attempting to rally as much support as possible, adopted the name of the man the members of the community revered as their founder.

If this theory is indeed accurate, the transition from reality to myth is not hard to surmise. The Sarmatian-Romans fought hard for a number of years, winning some battles and temporarily driving the invaders away. Artorius and his leading fighters, who would later be remembered as Arthur's knights, maintained their kingdom-like enclave until sometime in the sixth century, when the Saxons returned in force and finally overran the region. In the decades and centuries that followed, the memory of the natives' valiant stand, engineered by a war-leader named Arthur, passed through the generations, at first orally and later in writing, steadily mutating into myths that grew increasingly elaborate and embroidered over time.

Critics of this theory argue that many of the cultural elements relating to the Sarmatian-Arthurian connection—such as the warriors' lances and dragon banners—were not mentioned in any British writings before that of Geoffrey of Monmouth in the 1100s. This is true. However, the theory's

Celtic Versions of the Grail

The Holy Grail described in the Arthurian legends supposedly had magical powers, among them the ability to provide people with food or wealth or even to bring the dead back to life. The mystical object was not only a powerful Christian symbol, but also had characteristics associated with Celtic cauldrons, as pointed out by scholar Arthur Cotterell, former director of London's Kingston College.

When the Holy Grail, covered with a white cloth, appeared at Camelot, the vessel filled Arthur's hall with the most tasty smells, so that the knights of the Round Table ate and drank as never before. It was, in fact, nothing less than a Celtic cauldron of plenty. When, at the end of the Quest [for the Grail], the Grail became Christ's body, the draft [sip] that Sir Galahad took from it at Joseph of Arimathea's request ensured his spiritual survival. Like a Celtic cauldron of rebirth, it allowed Sir Galahad to live on in a Christian Otherworld [similar to the Otherworlds of Celtic mythology, where heroes lived after departing earth]. This obvious debt to Celtic mythology meant that the [Catholic] Church never fully embraced the Grail as a Christian symbol. The great popularity of the Grail stories forced a degree of toleration [by church authorities], but clerics were always aware of its links with pre-Christian rites.

Arthur Cotterell. *Celtic Mythology: The Myths and Legends of the Celtic World.* New York: Lorenz, 2000, p. 82.

The miraculous and magical Holy Grail was a powerful Christian symbol, but it actually had its roots in pagan myth.

The Arthurian legend may have had historical roots. The fifth-century Briton Artorius and his Sarmatian warriors (depicted here in battle) kept the invading Saxons at bay for years.

proponents counter, it is possible that Geoffrey and other later writers had access to documents or oral traditions that contained these elements but were subsequently lost.

An "Unquestionable Truth"

Even if the Sarmatian hypothesis is wrong, some strong parallels between the Arthurian myths and the abandoned residents of Britain in the fifth century are hard to deny. Those myths describe a brave, bold, honorable, and hardworking leader who arose from near obscurity in post-Roman England; defended the native population against invading enemies; and eventually faded from view, having acquired a lasting, highly favorable reputation. The real events, so far as historians currently understand them, were that following Rome's abandonment of Britain in the fifth century, at least some of the natives banded together, under one or more war leaders. They defended themselves against the encroaching Saxons and were successful for a time. But finally the invaders managed to overrun the region.

Another fact is that Arthur's legends began to form during and immediately after that pivotal period of British history—the fifth and sixth centuries. So it is not surprising that, mindful of the parallels listed above, numerous researchers have speculated that various historical figures from the period might have been the model for Arthur. In spite of their differences of opinion over the details, these scholars recognize a larger and "unquestionable truth," as Matthews terms it. "At the time when Britain faced a plunge into chaos and darkness," he says,

> a hero emerged who not only succeeded in getting the feuding tribes [of Roman Britain] to work together against their common enemy, but also led them in a series of smashing victories that established him as a figure of great power and importance—a figure ripe for developing into the myth-laden king of later accounts. . . . His legend began to grow almost immediately, as it continues to grow today, gathering ever more extraordinary and amazing details.[39]

CHAPTER 5

British Mythology in Popular Culture

Although England is a modern industrialized nation, it and other parts of the British Isles have not lost their cultural connection to their mystical, mythic past. In part this is because the remains of medieval castles, altar stones set in place by primeval Celtic worshippers, and other artifacts of ancient Britain still abound in the rolling countryside outside the cities and towns. These relics of more mysterious times beckon to the residents of the modern world. They are forceful reminders that many of the myths of early Britain remain as potent and compelling today as they were to the folk who gathered around communal campfires to hear those tales told aloud by roving bards. As scholar Richard Jones puts it:

> A fantastical aura of mystery and magic hangs heavy over England. . . . As you travel through the timeless villages of the eerily beautiful . . . countryside, the spirit of Arthur haunts a landscape of ruined castles, ancient hill forts, and enchanted pools. . . . Add to all this an abundance of brooding stone circles and prehistoric remnants, and you have a potent brew of tangible history around which myth and legend have woven a tapestry of wonder that remains as vibrant today as ever it was in the past.[40]

Indeed, most of the surviving ancient tales of Celtic and Norse gods and Anglo-Saxon, Irish, Welsh, and Arthurian heroes seemingly refused to die. In an almost unrelenting torrent, they flowed forward through the centuries, working their way into every form of literature, art, and communication conceived by each succeeding age. As a result, modern popular culture in the Western world abounds with them. They loom in images on movie and television screens and in comic books and video games as well as on the printed page. Thunor, Beowulf, Arthur, Robin Hood, and numerous others live on, ageless and endlessly appealing, as they

Everywhere in Britain ancient Celtic altar stones and relics, such as these at Stonehenge, are daily reminders that the myths of early Britain are as compelling today as in the past.

continuously capture the imaginations of new generations of devoted admirers.

Return of the Old Gods

A good example of this phenomenon is the way successive generations of people in the nineteenth and twentieth centuries, both young and old, became hooked on the images and stories of the Norse and Anglo-Saxon gods. Particularly important in popularizing these old deities for modern British, American, and other Western audiences was renowned English artist and writer William Morris (1834–1896). He both translated and retold several of the classic myths of the Germanic gods, making them household names among the educated classes. Also important was the long poem *The Ballad of the White Horse* (1911) by English writer G.K. Chesterton. It describes the exploits of the Saxon king Alfred the

Selkies from the Sea

In addition to the numerous modern books, stories, movies, and games that have featured the gods and heroes of the Celtic myths, a few others have explored some of the stranger beings from Celtic mythology, including fairies and *selkies*. The latter were seal-like aquatic creatures that were said to sometimes shed their skin, grow legs, and live temporarily on land as humans. The 1994 film *The Secret of Roan Inish*, based on a novel by Rosalie K. Fry and directed by John Sayles, portrayed a modern family whose ancestors were *selkies*. Another movie that dealt with this subject was the 2000 Australian film *Selkie*. The protagonist, a young man, suddenly discovers that he is a *selkie* and struggles to deal with what he views as a disturbing development. Still another successful movie about *selkies* was the Irish production *Ondine*, released in 2009, about a fisherman (portrayed by Colin Farrell) who finds that a woman (played by Alicja Bachleda) living in his town is a *selkie*. In the end the fisherman marries her and keeps her secret.

Great and how the Anglo-Saxon gods, including Woden/Odin and Thunor/Thor, began to be supplanted by Christian images.

Later literature in this vein included some entertaining novels, one of the finest of which was noted science-fiction and fantasy writer Poul Anderson's *The Broken Sword* (1954). Various anglicized Norse deities appear in its exciting plot about a half elf marrying an English queen in ancient Britain. Also, another popular fiction writer, Lester del Rey, explores the great battle among the Norse and Anglo-Saxon gods, Ragnarok, in his 1959 novel *The Day of the Giants*.

Meanwhile, the character Thor appears in hundreds of comic books put out by Marvel Comics. The renowned Marvel team of Stan Lee and Jack Kirby, veterans of the Fantastic Four comics, made Thor a member of the Avengers, a group of superheroes whose first adventures appeared in 1963. Lee and Kirby's Thor character was a sensation and over time appeared in spinoffs ranging from novels to TV programs, from role-playing to video games, and finally to the major 2011 feature film *Thor*, directed by Kenneth Branagh and featuring Chris Hemsworth in the title role.

The Many Versions of Beowulf

Another hero of British mythology, the Anglo-Saxon monster slayer Beowulf, has also enjoyed a new lease on life in modern popular culture. The late American novelist John Gardner cleverly retold Beowulf's tale from the point of view of the monster, Grendel, in the aptly titled *Grendel* (1971). In a plot that describes the title character's many raids on human habitations before Beowulf came along, Gardner explored the meaning of good and evil and the power of myths in human society.

The tale of Beowulf has also been adapted in a number of motion pictures. One was the 1999 film *Beowulf*, with French actor Christopher Lambert (best known for playing Tarzan) in the title role. That same year also saw the release of the highly entertaining epic *The 13th Warrior*, which partly depicts the true-life adventures of the medieval Arab traveler Ibn Fadlan. In the fictional section of the story,

Surpassing Tolkien?

Poul Anderson's *The Broken Sword* features a number of mythical races and other plot elements that are similar to those in J.R.R. Tolkien's world-famous *The Fellowship of the Ring,* the first volume of his *Lord of the Rings* trilogy. Michael Moorcock, a respected science-fiction and fantasy writer in his own right, considers Anderson's book to be superior to Tolkien's.

the traveler reaches the realm of King Hrothgar, who is of course the monarch from *Beowulf* who has been plagued by Grendel's attacks. In this version the monster's role is played by a tribe of cannibals called the Wendol (a play on the name Grendel). Other recent film versions of *Beowulf* include *Beowulf and Grendel* (2005); the made-for-TV *Grendel* (2007); a DVD titled *Beowulf* (2007), in which the actors speak Old English (aided by optional modern English subtitles); and the computer-animated *Beowulf* (2007).

The Formidable Forest Hero

Even more popular have been the plentiful modern retellings and spinoffs of the Robin Hood tales. After the emergence of the widely admired late medieval ballads about the formidable forest hero and his band of Merry Men, new literary versions appeared frequently. At first they were confined to Britain. But eventually they spread to other parts of Europe, as well as North America and beyond. These became so numerous, diverse, and widely distributed that no one could keep track of them all.

Fortunately for the many Robin Hood enthusiasts across the Western world, a diligent English lawyer, literary researcher, and writer named Joseph Ritson (1752–1803) came to the fore. A dedicated Robin Hood buff himself, he traveled widely and collected large numbers of old manuscripts, poems, ballads, and stories about the character. In 1795 Ritson published a hefty anthology of these materials titled *Robin Hood: A Collection of All the Ancient Poems, Songs, and Ballads Now Extant Relative to That Celebrated Outlaw.* Also included in the collection was the author's detailed version of the life of Robin, based on sections of the writings he had gathered.

Hundreds of modern writers, artists, filmmakers, and other Robin Hood fans later benefited greatly from Ritson's efforts. "This was the first comprehensive collection of references, ballads, and opinions on Robin Hood," remarks popular Robin Hood researcher Tony Wait. "There was scarcely a reference in literature to the outlaw that he didn't discover. . . . The book was hugely popular and everybody [interested in writing about Robin Hood] plundered it for ideas, references, and narratives."[41]

Among those plunderers were a slew of talented novelists, including the great Scottish writer Walter Scott (1771–1832). His groundbreaking, masterful work *Ivanhoe* (1819) is often credited as one of the major inspirations for modern interest in the medieval era, as well as the first great historical novel. The story traces the exploits of a Saxon noble, Wilfred of Ivanhoe, in England in the 1190s. He remains loyal to King Richard I, who is held hostage in Austria following the Third

Joseph Ritson collected old manuscripts, poems, ballads, and stories about Robin Hood, which he published in 1795.

Crusade. Richard eventually gains his freedom, returns to England, and, with the aid of Robin Hood and his outlaw companions, helps Ivanhoe overcome their mutual enemies. Scott's portrayal of Robin as a noble, just, and at times jovial person became the standard for the character ever after.

Later important novels about Robin Hood included Alexandre Dumas's *The Prince of Thieves* (1872) and its sequel, *Robin Hood the Outlaw* (1873); Howard Pyle's spirited *The Merry Adventures of Robin Hood* (1883); Rosemary Sutcliff's splendid *Chronicles of Robin Hood* (1950); Robin McKinley's *The Outlaws of Sherwood* (1988); Parke Godwin's atmospheric *Sherwood* (1991) and *Robin and the King* (1993); and Clayton Emery's *Robin Hood and the Beasts of Sherwood* (2002).

Sir Walter Scott's novel Ivanhoe *was published in 1819 and credited with inspiring a modern interest in the medieval myths.*

Robin Hood in Other Mediums

Equally noteworthy have been the many film adaptations of the Robin Hood legends. They include more than fifty feature films, at least fifteen animated productions, plus no less than fourteen TV series. Of the latter, particularly successful and popular was *The Adventures of Robin Hood*, a British series that ran from 1955 to 1960 (in the United States and other countries as well as in Britain). It starred the amiable British film actor Richard Greene as Robin.

Probably the most famous of the feature films about Robin Hood was the colorful and highly entertaining 1938 Hollywood version starring Australian actor Errol Flynn, who was known for his swashbuckling roles. But the big-screen version that many Robin Hood fans see as the most authentic and true to the original legends was the 1952 film *The Story of Robin Hood and His Merrie Men*, produced by Walt Disney. It starred the then dashing young British actor Richard Todd as Robin and Joan Rice as his love interest, Maid Marian. "*The Story of Robin Hood* is an eminently satisfying film," noted movie critic Leonard Maltin says while summing up the film's appeal.

> It takes all the familiar elements of the story—the confrontation between Robin and Little John on a wooden bridge over a stream, the archery tournament, the climactic duel—and plays them out with such gusto that one forgets ever having seen them before. There are delightful variations as well. Robin and his men communicate with each other by shooting whistling arrows throughout the forest—different arrows producing different pitches, and thus signifying different things. . . . The performances are uniformly fine, with an impressive roster of talented players. James Robertson Justice as Little John and Peter Finch as the wicked Sheriff stand out. . . . This is an extremely good-*looking* film as well. The locations are beautiful, with lush green countrysides; the sets are truly formidable and realistic.[42]

Robin Hood in Comics

One of the more widely popular illustrated versions of Robin Hood and his exploits was created by the British company Thriller Comics. The series ran from 1951 to 1963 and included some 450 issues in all.

A recent film version of the legend of Robin Hood was Ridley Scott's 2010 film Robin Hood, *starring Russell Crowe in the title role.*

Among the other modern visual mediums in which Robin Hood has appeared are comic books and various sorts of games. The much beloved Classic Comics series of the early to mid-1900s released a beautiful rendition of his legends. It first appeared in 1942 and by popular demand was reprinted in 1946, 1955, 1964 to 1967, and 1969. Also, the British company Thriller Comics issued a long series of Robin Hood comic books beginning in 1951. Meanwhile, at least twelve board and card games and almost twenty video games based on Robin's myths have hit the market over the years.

The Arthurian Treasure Trove

Perhaps not surprisingly, the only mythical British figure who has generated more modern cultural adaptations than Robin Hood is King Arthur. Malory's pivotal *Le Morte d'Arthur*, which was itself partially the product of numerous earlier Arthurian works, in turn served as the inspiration for seemingly countless early modern and modern versions. Of the latter, one of the most famous and well liked is Englishman Alfred Lord Tennyson's series of long poems *Idylls of the King*, completed in 1874.

Published in sections over the course of several years, the work is a detailed retelling of the principal Arthurian legends. Overall, the plot is similar to Malory's. However, Tennyson placed more stress on social values that were current

Robin's Video Adventures

In addition to poems, novels, movies, TV shows, and comic books, the Robin Hood myths inspired numerous video games. One of the first was *The Adventures of Robin Hood*, released by Millennium Interactive in 1991. The object of the game was to help the hero, identified here as Robin of Loxley, get back into his castle, which had been seized by the villainous sheriff of Nottingham. (Although the game's cover featured a photo of Kevin Costner as Robin from the feature film *Robin Hood: Prince of Thieves*, the game did not follow the movie's plot.) Much more complex was the 2003 game *Robin Hood: Defender of the Crown*, made for PlayStation 2 and Xbox. In this version the player followed Robin through all sorts of adventures, including robbing the rich, sword fighting, jousting on horseback, and laying siege to castles. Some of the other video games starring Robin Hood were *Robin Hood: Legend Quest* (Codemasters, 1993), *Robin Hood* (EA/Light & Shadow, 2001), and *Robin Hood: The Legend of Sherwood* (Wanadoo, 2002).

White's King Arthur

T.H. White's widely acclaimed retelling of the Arthurian legends, *The Once and Future King,* consists of four sections—The Sword in the Stone, about Arthur's background and rise to the kingship; The Queen of Air and Darkness, covering the early years of his reign in Camelot; The Ill-Made Knight, recounting the adventures of Sir Lancelot; and The Candle in the Wind, telling of the fall of Camelot and tragic end of Arthur's reign and dreams.

in his own time—Britain's Victorian era, or the years dominated by the reign of Queen Victoria (1837–1901). Victorian literature tended to be romantic (in the sentimental and idealistic sense). In the *Idylls* this was exemplified by the author's emphasis on courtly love and expectations of strict moral behavior by Arthur, his knights, and especially Guinevere. Accordingly, Tennyson laid a large portion of the blame for Camelot's fall on the queen's infidelity, here seen as betrayal not only of her husband but also of the high-minded ideals he had set for himself and his realm.

In addition to Tennyson's work, the Victorian era generated a virtual treasure trove of Arthurian popular culture, especially artistic spin-offs. "Throughout the Victorian era," John Matthews recalls,

> Arthurian themes dominated the arts of poetry, music, and painting. The Pre-Raphaelite Brotherhood [a group of famous painters], whose numbers included Dante Gabriel Rossetti, Edward Burne-Jones, and William Morris, produced striking paintings based on Arthurian themes. One of the earliest photographers, Julia Margaret Cameron, produced a series of portraits of scenes from Tennyson's poems in which well-known people posed as Arthurian characters. Poetry, good, bad, and indifferent, imitating Tennyson, poured forth and was avidly read. Plays and pageants were performed all over the country depicting the adventures of Arthur and his knights. The magic and beauty of the stories wove a spell over the drab Victorian age, touching again and again on the deepest levels of human experience.[43]

In many ways English writer T.H. White's 1958 novel *The Once and Future King* was for the twentieth century what Tennyson's *Idylls* had been for the nineteenth century.

White's reinterpretation of several of the characters, rendering them more complex and in some ways more modern than in earlier versions, became tremendously influential in subsequent Arthurian adaptations. Among these spinoffs were the delightful 1960 hit Broadway musical *Camelot* (starring Richard Burton as Arthur and Julie Andrews as Guinevere); its 1967 movie version (with Richard Harris and Vanessa Redgrave in the lead roles); and Walt Disney's feature-length cartoon *The Sword in the Stone* (1965), based on part one of White's book.

The Sword in the Stone and Camelot were neither the first nor the last of the film versions of the Arthurian myths. There had already been multiple movies made of iconic American humorist Mark Twain's witty novel *A Connecticut Yankee in*

The 2004 film King Arthur *about the Arthurian legend has Clive Owen (center surrounded by his knights) as Artorius, fighting Saxon invaders.*

Justice in an Imperfect World?

King Arthur is no less popular in the United States than he is in Britain. Large numbers of American novels, scholarly volumes, Broadway shows, musical pieces, films, video games, Internet sites, college courses, and toys based on the Arthurian legends have appeared over the years. This proves that these centuries-old myths are as alive today as they were when they first came into being in Britain long ago. In part this may be because in an imperfect world Arthur has come to symbolize many people's inner desires for the just, morally upright society he supposedly created. In the words of literary scholar Christopher Snyder, "Camelot still speaks to us. As [the late British leader] Winston Churchill asserted, [the King Arthur mythos is] a lasting and important part of our Western cultural inheritance, like the stories of Homer and the Bible, to be drawn upon whenever we want to express our societal hopes and fears. 'It is all true,' wrote Churchill of the Arthurian legends, 'or it ought to be.'"

Christopher Snyder. *The World of King Arthur*. London: Thames and Hudson, 2000, p. 177.

The Arthurian legend has endured because it has come to symbolize many people's inner desires for a just, morally sound society.

King Arthur's Court. They included a 1921 silent version; the first sound adaptation (1931), starring another renowned humorist, Will Rogers; and a musical version (1949), featuring popular singer-actor Bing Crosby. There were also many colorful adventure films about Arthur, his knights, and the sorcerer Merlin, among them *Knights of the Round Table* (1953), *Prince Valiant* (1954), *The Sword of Lancelot* (1963), *Arthur of the Britons* (1972), *Monty Python and the Holy Grail* (1975), *Excalibur* (1981), *Merlin and the Dragons* (1991, animated), *A Kid in King Arthur's Court* (1995), *Merlin* (1998, TV miniseries), *The Mists of Avalon* (2001), and *King Arthur* (2004).

A Timeless Quality

These very partial lists of the myriad movies, TV series, poems, novels, plays, musical pieces, comic books, games, and other spinoffs of the ancient and medieval British myths testify to the strong appeal of the original versions. On one level, they were wonderful slices of entertainment. On another, they reflected the personal instincts and concerns of the peoples who produced them.

Finally, the ancient myths possessed a timeless quality that has made their already countless adaptations attractive, engaging, and successful. Some of Arthur's tales claim he will someday return. Similarly, the major British myths will almost surely continue to return in new, sometimes surprising, and always fascinating forms for as long as Western civilization exists.

NOTES

Introduction: A Rich, Diverse Mythical Heritage

1. Geoffrey Ashe. *Mythology of the British Isles*. New York: Methuen, 2002, p. 106.
2. Richard Barber. *Myths and Legends of the British Isles*. New York: Barnes and Noble, 2004, p. 23.
3. Christopher R. Fee. *Gods, Heroes, and Kings: The Battle for Mythic Britain*. New York: Oxford University Press, 2004, p. 7.
4. Richard Jones. *Myths and Legends of Britain and Ireland*. London: New Holland, 2003, p. 10.
5. Fee. *Gods, Heroes, and Kings*, p. 8.
6. Ashe. *Mythology of the British Isles*, p. 9.
7. Barber. *Myths and Legends of the British Isles*, p. 34.

Chapter 1: Myths Born of a Clash of Cultures

8. Fee. *Gods, Heroes, and Kings*, p. ix.
9. Julius Caesar. *Commentaries*. Published as *War Commentaries of Caesar*. Translated by Rex Warner. New York: Plume, 1987, pp. 123–124.
10. Quoted in Henry Loyn. *The Vikings in Britain*. Hoboken, NJ: Wiley-Blackwell, 1995, pp. 55–56.
11. BBC. "Christianity in Britain." www.bbc.co.uk/religion/religionschristianity/history/uk_1.shtml.
12. Fee. *Gods, Heroes, and Kings*, p. 9.

Chapter 2: Tales of the Ancient British Gods

13. Fee. *Gods, Heroes, and Kings*, p. 14.
14. Peter Berresford Ellis. *Celtic Myths and Legends*. New York: Carroll and Graf, 2004, p. 21.
15. Ellis. *Celtic Myths and Legends*, p. 329.
16. Ellis. *Celtic Myths and Legends*, p. 330.
17. Ashe. *Mythology of the British Isles*, pp. 92–93.
18. Ellis. *Celtic Myths and Legends*, p. 20.
19. Miranda J. Green. *Celtic Myths*. Austin: University of Texas Press, 1993, p. 14.
20. Dio Cassius. *Roman History*, Book 62. Translated by Ernest Cary. www.brainfly.net/html/books/diocas62.htm.

Chapter 3: Legends of Beloved Human Heroes

21. M.I. Ebbutt. *Hero-Myths and Legends of the British Race*. Calgary, AB: Theophania, 2011, pp. xiv–xv.

22. Chris Vinsonhaler. "Teaching Resources." Beowulf Poet.com. www.beowulfpoet.com/TEAelements.html.
23. Quoted in Barber. *Myths and Legends of the British Isles*, pp. 203–204.
24. Quoted in Barber. *Myths and Legends of the British Isles*, p. 202.
25. Quoted in Barber. *Myths and Legends of the British Isles*, p. 90.
26. Quoted in Barber. *Myths and Legends of the British Isles*, p. 90.
27. Quoted in Barber. *Myths and Legends of the British Isles*, p. 90.
28. Quoted in Barber. *Myths and Legends of the British Isles*, p. 37.
29. From the theme song of the 1950s British TV show *The Adventures of Robin Hood*. Quoted in Alan W. Wright. "The Adventures of Robin Hood: A Robin Hood Spotlight." Robin Hood: Bold Outlaw of Barnsdale and Sherwood. www.boldoutlaw.com/robspot/greenerobin.html.
30. Quoted in Thomas G. Hahn. *Robin Hood in Popular Culture*. Suffolk, England: Boydell, 2000, p. 127.
31. Mike Ibeji. "Robin Hood and His Historical Context." BBC. www.bbc.co.uk/history/british/middle_ages/robin_01.shtml.

Chapter 4: Britain's Most Popular Character

32. Graham Phillips and Martin Keatman. *King Arthur: The True Story*. London: Century Random House, 1992, p. 3.
33. Thomas Malory. *Le Morte d'Arthur*. Published as *King Arthur and His Knights of the Round Table*. Edited by Sidney Lanier. New York: Atheneum, 1989, p. 4.
34. Malory. *Le Morte d'Arthur*, p. 7.
35. Quoted in Britannia. "A Conversation with Geoffrey Ashe." www.britannia.com/history/h17.html.
36. Philip Wilkinson. *The Illustrated Dictionary of Mythology*. New York: Dorling Kindersley, 1998, p. 92.
37. Quoted in Britannia. "A Conversation with Geoffrey Ashe."
38. John Matthews. *King Arthur: Dark Age Warrior and Mythic Hero*. New York: Random House, 2004, p. 22.
39. Matthews. *King Arthur*, p. 23.

Chapter 5: British Mythology in Popular Culture

40. Jones. *Myths and Legends of Britain and Ireland*, p. 14.
41. Tony Wait. "Joan Rice." *Walt Disney's Robin Hood* (blog). http://disneysrobin.blogspot.com/2009_10_01_archive.html.
42. Leonard Maltin. *The Disney Films*. New York: Hyperion, 1995, pp. 236–237.
43. Matthews. *King Arthur*, pp. 108–109.

anthropomorphism: Assigning human characteristics to animals or objects.

bard: A poet or storyteller.

cauldron: A large metal pot used for cooking or boiling water.

comitatus: The ancient Germanic heroic code, a set of rules that Norse and Anglo-Saxon warriors were expected to follow.

Druid: An ancient Celtic holy man.

hall: In medieval Europe, a large structure in which a ruler and his nobles met, held court, and/or feasted.

Holy Grail: In British mythology, the cup used by Jesus at the Last Supper.

mythos: A large collection of myths and related beliefs and customs surrounding a legendary person, place, or people.

pantheon: A group of gods worshipped by a people or nation.

persona: The character or personality someone displays.

Ragnarok: In Norse and Anglo-Saxon mythology, the "twilight of the gods," or final battle between the gods and their enemies; it was believed that the gods would lose.

romance: In medieval Europe, a long story written in prose.

sacrifice: An offering or gift made to a god or gods.

swashbuckling: Having to do with themes such as adventure and romance, especially including heroic characters who fight with swords and other old-fashioned weapons.

venerate: To worship or hold in high esteem.

Books

Geoffrey Ashe. *Mythology of the British Isles*. New York: Methuen, 2002. An excellent exploration of the myths of the Celts, Saxons, and other early British peoples, including the backgrounds of those tales.

Richard Barber. *Myths and Legends of the British Isles*. New York: Barnes and Noble, 2004. A comprehensive collection of ancient British myths, including those of the Saxons, Welsh, Irish, and other early British peoples.

Nora K. Chadwick and Barry Cunliffe. *The Celts*. London: Folio Society, 2008. The authors have compiled one of the best available overviews of Celtic culture, told in easy-to-read prose.

Arthur Cotterell. *Celtic Mythology: The Myths and Legends of the Celtic World*. New York: Lorenz, 2000. This first-rate introductory mythology book features an encyclopedia-style, alphabetical listing of mythical characters, supported by many beautiful color illustrations.

H.R.E. Davidson. *Gods and Myths of Northern Europe*. Baltimore: Penguin, 1984. One of the best general overviews of Norse, Anglo-Saxon, and other northern European beliefs and myths, written by one of the acknowledged experts in the field.

Peter Berresford Ellis. *Celtic Myths and Legends*. New York: Carroll and Graf, 2004. This is one of the most comprehensive collections of old Celtic myths available today.

Cheryl Evans and Anne Millard. *Usborne Illustrated Guide to Norse Myths and Legends*. London: Usborne, 1994. Aimed at younger readers, this beautiful, information-packed volume about Norse myths, which were integral to early British culture, will also appeal to general adult readers.

Christopher R. Fee. *Gods, Heroes, and Kings: The Battle for Mythic Britain*. New York: Oxford University Press, 2004. The author presents a well-written, detailed exposition of the divine pantheons, heroes, and sacred objects of the Celts, Scandinavians, and other peoples who contributed tales to the mythology of ancient Britain.

Patrick K. Ford, ed. and trans. *The Mabinogi and Other Medieval Welsh Tales*. Berkeley: University of California Press, 2008. This is a highly regarded translation of some of the old Welsh tales that will appeal to all buffs of British history and mythology.

Miranda J. Green. *Celtic Myths*. Austin: University of Texas Press, 1993. A straightforward, easy-to-read compilation of the major Celtic myths and legendary characters.

J.C. Holt. *Robin Hood*. London: Thames and Hudson, 2011. One of the best modern examinations of the Robin Hood legends, this book by a distinguished medieval historian explores the major theories about the character's possible authenticity.

Richard Jones. *Myths and Legends of Britain and Ireland*. London: New Holland, 2003. A beautifully illustrated volume that explores the various settings of the old myths of Britain and Ireland. The text is also first rate and easy to read.

Rosalind Kerven. *DK Classics: King Arthur*. London: Dorling Kindersley, 1998. A handsomely illustrated introduction to the Arthurian characters and legends, aimed at young readers.

Magnus Magnusson. *Hammer of the North: Myths and Heroes of the Viking Age*. New York: Putnam, 1986. A very useful examination of the major Viking myths and heroes.

Graham Phillips and Martin Keatman. *King Arthur: The True Story*. London: Century Random House, 1999. This highly informative volume provides an overview of the various theories that contend that the Arthurian legends were based on at least some real characters.

Howard Pyle. *The Adventures of Robin Hood*. New York: Sterling, 2005. This is a recent reprint of the classic telling of the Robin Hood myths by the great American storyteller and illustrator Howard Pyle (1853–1911).

Christopher Snyder. *The World of King Arthur*. London: Thames and Hudson, 2000. A well-written and exquisitely illustrated overview of Arthurian history, lore, literature, and more.

Richard White, ed. *King Arthur in Legend and History*. London: Routledge, 1990. A large and extremely useful compendium of primary Arthurian documents, including excerpts or full texts of various historical as well as literary works concerning Arthur, his knights, Camelot, and so forth.

Websites

Beowulf, **Internet Sacred Text Archive** (http://sacred-texts.com/neu/eng/hml/hml05.htm). M.I. Ebbutt's classic telling of the Beowulf myth, one of the major hero legends of ancient Britain.

Celtic Gods and Goddesses (www.belaterreno.com/graphics/clipart_mystical/celticgods/default.htm). A colorful collection of images created over the centuries that depict the various deities of Celtic mythology.

Dream of Rhonabwy, Britannia (www.britannia.com/history/docs/rhonabwy.html). A translation of part of the famous early Welsh tale that pictures Arthur without Camelot and his other royal trappings.

Holy Grail, Britannia (www.britannia.com/history/arthur/grail.html). An excellent introduction to the Holy Grail, one of the chief mystical elements of the Arthurian myths.

Merlin, Camelot Project at the University of Rochester (www.lib.rochester .edu/Camelot/rwemerl1.htm; www .lib.rochester.edu/Camelot/rwemerl2 .htm). These sites contain the verses about the mythical British character Merlin that were composed by the well-known nineteenth-century poet Ralph Waldo Emerson.

Search for the Real Robin Hood (http:// boldoutlaw.com/realrob/index.html). Allen W. Wright's excellent explorations into the various theories of who the real Robin Hood was—*if* he was a real person.

Religion
  Anglo-Saxon, 26–27
  Celtic, 21–22
  See also Christianity
Ritson, Joseph, 88–89, *89*
River Styx, 44, *44*
Robin Hood, 32, 61–65, *62*, *63*, *64*,
  89
  in films, 91, *92*
  in literature, 88–90
  in video games, 92, 93
Robin Hood and the Monk (ballad),
  63
Robin Hood (film), *92*
Rochester Castle, *32*
Roman Britain, 14–15, 25–26
  map of, *6*
Roman mythology, 26
  interaction between Celtic
    mythology and, 41–44

S

Sarmatian-Romans, 79–80
Sarmatians/Sarmatian warriors, 79,
  82
Scott, Walter, 89, *90*
Scythia, 79
The Secret of Roan Inish (film), 86
Selkie (film), 86
Selkies (mythological creatures),
  86
Shakespeare, William, 12, 58
Sherwood (Godwin), 90

St. Cuthbert's Church, 28, 29
Stonehenge, 27, *27*, 85
*The Story of Robin Hood and His
  Merrie Men* (film), 91
Sutcliff, Rosemary, 90
The Sword in the Stone (film),
  95
Sword in the stone myth, 70–73,
  79–80

T

Tennyson, Alfred Lord, 93–94
Thetis (Greek nymph), 44, *44*
The 13th Warrior (film), 87–88
Thor (film), 87
Thor (Norse god), 47
Thunor (Anglo-Saxon deity), 27,
  46–49, *47*
Tolkien, J.R.R., 88
Tristan (knight), *67*
Tuatha (deities), 44

U

Uther Pendragon, 68–69, *69*, 79

V

Vanir (Norse deities), 45
Video games, 92, 93
Vikings (Norsemen), *28*, 28–30,
  48
Villages, prehistoric, 19, *19*

Virgil (Roman poet), 15
Viviane (Lady of the Lake), 74
Vulcan (Roman deity), 43

W

Wallace, William, 32
Waterways, magical, 44, *44*
Welsh Annals (*Annales Cambriae*),
   68, 70

Wen (Anglo-Saxon deities), 45
White, T.H., 94–95
William the Conqueror, 30
Winchester Castle, *78*
Woden (Anglo-Saxon deity), 27

Y

Ysbaddaden (chief of giants),
   56–57, 58

PICTURE CREDITS

Historian Don Nardo has written numerous acclaimed volumes about ancient civilizations and peoples. Among these are studies of the religious beliefs and myths of those peoples, including the Greeks, Romans, Egyptians, Sumerians, and others. Nardo also composes and arranges orchestral music. He resides with his wife, Christine, in Massachusetts.